WORKER PARTICIPATION

PRESCRIPTION FOR INDUSTRIAL CHANGE

Frank R. Anton

University of Calgary

Detselig Enterprises Limited

Calgary, Alberta

Frank R. Anton
Professor of Economics
University of Calgary

© 1980 by Detselig Enterprises Limited
6147 Dalmarnock Cr. N.W.
Calgary, Alberta T3A 1H3

Printed in Canada   ISBN 0-920490-07-7

Contents

Preface

In common with most other industrial economies during the 1950's and 1960's the Canadian economy demonstrated a fairly steady growth rate and a surprising degree of flexibility which enabled it to accommodate the innumerable economic, political and social changes which were thrust upon it by both internal and external forces. But with the emergence of "stagflation" in the 1970's there is evidence that the rate of growth in output and, more significantly, productivity have tended to decelerate and that the competitive edge once held by industries in the primary and secondary sectors is gradually being eroded by the superior efficiency of competitor industries in other countries. How much of this deterioration is due to a decline in the rate of investment in new plant and equipment, research and development and innovations (hastened perhaps by inappropriate taxation policies) is difficult to determine. What is determinate however, is the thoroughly unsatisfactory state of labour-management relations in Canada as evidenced, during the past decade, by the second worst work-stoppage record among the industrial nations of the world. That industrial conflict impedes efficient production is self-evident. Less well known and recognized are its deleterious consequences on unit labour cost, prices, profits and employment. The sequential links between these are fairly precise: if wage increases exceed average gains in productivity, unit labour costs must rise and, in the absence of protective tariffs or quotas, stagflation in the form of unacceptably high prices and unemployment results. At issue therefore is the system of wage (and fringe benefit) determination followed in Canada which has led to excessive industrial conflict and rising unit labour cost relative to the more innovative approaches of certain other countries where work-stoppages are the exception rather than the norm.

The Canadian approach to wage/salary/fringe benefit negotiations - in both the private and public sectors - may be described as primarily adversarial. Negotiators bargain over how available, or sometimes shrinking, revenues are to be divided and how managements' drive for productive efficiency and workers' quest for job, income and psychic security are to be reconciled. The European approach is the obverse of this: it seeks for ways and means to increase revenues by more efficient methods of production and avoidance of strikes so that a bigger product is available for sharing. Moreover, unlike North America where the labour-management function is usually relegated to a secondary role, except during annual or bi-annual collective bargaining rituals, specific laws require that it be given top *and* continuous priority including provision for employees to participate in work-place decisions. In return for this recognition and responsibility workers usually accept a commitment to the enterprise which brings rewards to management and labour alike.

Management and labour adhering to the adversarial approach should not be surprised that industrial conflict is heightened and intensified particularly in times of rising prices and unemployment. Many impartial observers of this phenomenon, consider it unnecessary and assert that it stems, in the main, from an outmoded industrial relations system designed to resolve conflict through conflict. The time has therefore come not only for an upgrading of the industrial relations function but also for a complete overhaul of the total system in order that the participants can better cope with the technological revolution facing them in the years ahead. Among the many suggestions for achieving this is one deserving of close and urgent attention, namely, acceptance of a system of worker participation - or industrial democracy - whereby employees are encouraged to have a say in important aspects of managerial decision-making which were previously considered as exclusivve managerial prerogatives.

The mere act of adopting some form of worker participation in Canada will not, in itself, be a panacea for all, or most, of the labour-management problems besetting the economy. On the contrary, its adoption will raise problems for both sides but there is little doubt that the opportunities and benefits it offers far exceed the costs. Unfortunately, there is a great deal of misunderstanding of what worker participation is all about. It is not, as many think, a means whereby uninterested trade unions and reluctant employers are compelled to accept worker directors in the enterprise. This, on its own, would be a pointless exercise. But it is a means of getting workers involved that is rewarding to both employers and employees. For this reason it deserves careful study. As pointed out recently in *The Economist*, adoption of worker participation means change; above all a change of attitudes without which a change of mechanisms may do more harm than good. Change brings its own problems "but the rewards of an involved and therefore committed workforce can be great - as can the harm done by a workforce which continues to be denied the chance to be either.''

Almost without exception evidence from West European employers and unions attest to the merits of worker participation - despite its difficulties. Few apparently would wish to function without it. But it is emphasised that participation imposed solely at, or from, the top is unworkable whereas it can be invaluable lower down. West Germany's experience suggests that works councils (rather than worker directors) contribute most to make that system work. Can Canadian labour and management be induced to learn from this example?

Most North American employers tend to reject the concept of "worker participation" or "industrial democracy" mainly because they visualize it leading to the workplace being run by committee. If convinced it were profitable they would probably accept it. Acceptance of the principle that employees are entitled to a say in company decisions has merit. After all employees have a closer and more important stake in their jobs than that of most shareholders who, in any event, can sell out if they dislike the way the business is being run. As the exciting challenges of the 1980's arise (particularly with the increasing use of micro-processors) the best response is to have a responsible workforce. This can be achieved by treating it responsibly.

The successes attributed to the various systems of worker participation, particularly in those countries where they have received widespread adoption, are impressive. The purpose of this study is therefore to promote discussion of this highly controversial issue. To ignore such an innovation without proposing acceptable alternatives to existing Canadian practices, may imperil our economy. The hope is that all those involved in Canadian industry - management, labour, *and* government - will find the ideas contained in this study sufficiently challenging and provocative to give them serious consideration.

I am indebted to the Department of Energy, Mines and resources for the financial assistance given me to undertake this work. I owe a special debt of gratitude to Miss Janice Cheslak, a graduate student in the Department of Economics, for her painstaking and valuable research assistance.

F.R. Anton
Department of Economics
University of Calgary
January 1980.

7

I

General Philosophy Underlying Worker Participation

The notion that workers should participate in the management of the enterprises which employ them is not new. It has apparently existed since the beginnings of the industrial revolution when individuals became separated from the direction of their work.[1] However, worker participation is currently receiving unprecedented interest as a viable approach to meeting a changing industrial relations environment. Although countries' economic-political-social contexts vary widely, certain long run forces common to most Western industrial societies are tending to produce a change in attitudes towards the nature of work and the role of the enterprise. Many countries are experiencing a demand for greater worker involvement in management decisions and there is a growing desire for extension of personal freedom at work. Moreover, the structure of the enterprise itself is undergoing change in numerous countries, as evidenced by modification of company laws, greater powers given to workers or their representative institutions, and acceptance of new forms of relationships between labour, management and governments.[2]

This chapter will investigate the fundamental causes of these changing attitudes leading to a transformation of traditional labour-management relations and the concept of worker participation as one approach to accommodating the new situation.

9

Causes of Recent Changes in Labour-Management Relations

N. F. Dufty has proposed a useful model for analysing the causes of recent changes in our industrial relations systems and the implications for the concept of worker participation.[3] Basically, the model consists of an enviromental and an industrial relations system wherein the particular technological, economic, and social sub-systems impinge upon the values of the actors in an industrial relations system, namely the workers, unions and management.[4] The values, as well as the relative power of the actors, determine the character of the industrial relations system. The model is interactive where a change in one component will create a reaction in all the others.[5] In terms of the present analysis, it would appear that particular evolutions in the technological, economic and social sub-systems have initiated a revaluation of attitudes and a general questioning of established labour-management relations.

A. THE ENVIRONMENT

1. Technological Sub-System

Technological change is a potent source of changes in labour-management relations, particularly as it influences the nature of work itself and the balance of power between the actors.[6] During the post war period industrial enterprises have experienced rapid technological change with increased specialization of jobs, growth in the size and complexity of their organizations and a movement towards more centralized decision-making.[7] Although these changes have produced great economic benefits in terms of rising productivity levels and standards of living, there has also been the creation of some social costs. Resultant claims include fragmentation and rationalization which frequently transform relatively autonomous and skilled tasks into lower quality "impoverised" work.[8] While technological change tends to reduce the physical demands of work, it may actually increase mental stress, ". . . as man meets the requirements of the machine rather than the machine responding to man."[9] Furthermore, the emergence of large, complex organizations with a centralized authority structure has apparently contributed to a sense of meaninglessness, powerlessness, and isolation as the worker tends to lose sight of the whole work process and to feel dominated by the new technology.[10]

At the same time, technical changes may have altered the balance of power between labour and management. Intensive task specialization has tended to place small work groups in a powerful position where they have the potential of inflicting heavy losses on management through work stoppages. Indeed, Dufty argues that technical change is one of the principle determinants of labour-management relations due to its potential for changing the power relations.[11]

2. Economic Sub-Systems

It frequently has been noted that such positive economic factors as wider availability of comprehensive social security systems, high employment levels, and increasing financial reserves of the average worker have substantially reduced the "coercive necessity of work". In turn this has led to a rise in workers' expectations, more bargaining power vis-a-vis managment, and workers' willingness to use this power.[12] The growing number of work stoppages during the present inflationary period is possible evidence of workers' greater propensity to strike in an attempt to maintain their standards of living and reduce the distortion of perceived acceptable earnings differentials among various groups. This is particularly evident among the white collar workers who are increasingly turning to unionism in an effort to regain their traditional status and earnings position within the hierarchy.

3. Social Sub-System

By its nature, the social sub-system influences all the other environmental sub-systems and provides the main impact on the values of the actors in the industrial relations system.[13] Constantly rising educational levels and rapid communication of ideas through modern mass media techniques have been cited as two crucial forces which are changing individual's qualifications, viewpoints and aspirations.[14] A new generation is entering industry who have been instilled with the value of individual expression and who are used to being informed and consulted on important issues.[15] Moreover, the youth of numerous countries are attacking traditional life styles, questioning all forms of established authority structures. In particular, strong pressure is being exerted for more individual freedom and democracy to be extended to the work place.[16]

B.   THE INDUSTRIAL RELATIONS SYSTEM

The evolutions in the technological, economic and social sub-systems have tended to modify many traditional values inherent in our industrial societies. Following Dufty's approach, these changing values can be investigated under worker, union, and management ideologies.

1.   Worker Ideologies

Possibly as a result of rising educational levels, higher living standards, wider job choices and extensive information concerning alternative work practices, it is apparent that employees are demanding more meaningful work.[17] As individuals' quantitative needs are met, attention turns towards qualitative needs where it is argued, ". . . work viewed simply as a means of earning a living, with no consideration being given to questions of job satisfaction is no longer (if it ever was) accepted by rank and file workers."[18] These demands for increased job satisfaction may include improved working conditions, job enrichment, additional responsibility in work and better communications within the enterprise. Workers are also challenging traditional concepts of managerial authority and legitimacy. Pursuing their general desire for more individual freedom and democracy within society, employees are now tending to demand greater participation in the decision-making process of the enterprise. Hence, workers' expectations are changing with respect to their jobs and role in the enterprise - they are less inclined to accept decisions on trust and customary bases of authority.[19]

2.   Union Ideologies

It has been argued that most unions adopt an ideology which suits their purpose at hand, thus creating a set of notions that are rarely internally consistent.[20] Yet, unions generally have the common aim of maximizing labour's influence on management decisions. With enhanced bargaining power as a result of the recent economic and technological evolutions, unions in various countries are tending to apply greater pressure for, and obtain, additional participation rights.[21] This is evidenced in the growing scope of collective bargaining issues and establishment of labour representatives on management boards.

As union ideologies are highly influenced by the social sub-system, the specific methods adopted to affect managerial discretion may vary widely among countries. For example, the American trade union movement has generally maintained its traditional adversary philosophy where, ". . . the union wishes to be a critic rather that a partner in management. . . ", and does not wish to accept formal responsibility for the life of the enterprise.[22] Accordingly, greater participation is seen to be obtained through established collective bargaining machinery. In contrast, West German trade unions have adopted a philosophy of support for the success of the capitalist system and are willing to accept responsibility for their enterprises' prosperity. Consequently, they have pressed for partnership in decision-making at all levels of the organization, including supervisory board representation. Finally, whatever form is adopted, the recent inflationary period accompanied by rising levels of unemployment can be expected to intensify labour's efforts to gain more control over their lives within the enterprise.

3. Management Ideologies

The growth of large corporations and rising educational levels have tended to produce a professional class of management who view their function as a balancing force between the interests of the various stake holders in the company, namely the workers, customers, shareholders and suppliers.[23] Therefore, their values may no longer exactly coincide with those of the owners of capital. The appearance of professional managers has been termed the "second managerial revolution" with the first managerial revolution being the appearance of management itself as a specialized function within hierarchial organization.[24] Professional managers generally seem willing to accept greater worker participation as a means of involving or motivating workers and of legitimizing managerial authority. However, they usually resist any surrender of decision-making power on the grounds that their professional competence and decision-making freedom are essential for the efficient operation of the enterprise.[25]

Yet, despite managements' present reluctance to forego their established prerogatives, it has been noted that, ". . . management ideologies are subject to change under pressure and the success of workers or their organizations in modifying the decision-making structure will lead, in the course of time, to the modification of management ideologies."[26] There is some evidence of a current shift in ideology as a growing number of managers are accepting the idea that possibly the only way for management to retain control is to share it. In fact, it has been asserted that a "third managerial revolution" is in progress which embodies the principle of participation.[27]

C. IMPLICATIONS FOR WORKER PARTICIPATION

The above evolutions in the technological, economic and social sub-systems with their resulting impact on ideologies have significantly affected labour-management relations. There appears to be redefinition occurring concerning the role, function and responsibility of the enterprise in the western industrial societies.[28] The enterprise is now seen to have a social value of its own with multiple interests to serve those of the employees, the local and national community as well as those of the shareholders. Traditional divisions of labour and authority relationships within industry are being questioned. Generally rising levels of employee turnover, absenteeism, and growing industrial strife would seem to indicate that a large number of employees are not satisfied with their present industrial relations system. As R. K. Andras has perceived, "There may well be an inherent conflict between the capabilities and demands of increasingly well-educated labour forces and the apparently increasingly narrow set of functions that we give individuals to perform."[29]

Thus, it is commonly agreed there is a need for both management and labour to devise new organizational and decision-making structures which would increase the social benefits of work while at the same time promoting economic efficiency. Although the necessary changes will tend to vary according to the nature of the industrial relations system and other institutions in a particular country, some form of worker participation is gaining support as a feasible approach for solving many of those issues.

The Concept of Worker Participation

The concept of worker participation is highly complex and controversial. In very general terms, it may be described as a situation in which workers have obtained or been given the right to take part in managerial decision-making.[30] However, worker participation has a variety of meanings depending upon the objectives or aims it is meant to achieve, the forms it takes, the range of issues subject to worker involvement, and the degree to which workers can influence management decisions. Therefore, these factors will be discussed to facilitate an understanding of the concept and its philosophy.

A. AIMS OF WORKER PARTICIPATION

Although numerous objectives have been attributed to worker participation, they may be divided into three broad classes according to the particular philosophy or school of thought adopted by the different proponents of participation. These aims are identified as ethical-psychological, politico-social, and economic.[31] This classification scheme is analogous to Edward S. Greenberg's delineation of four divergent schools of thought which are based on the different objectives that participation is expected to achieve. Thus, for example, the ethical-psychological, politico-social, and economic aims correspond respectively to Greenberg's Humanistic Psychology, Democratic Theory, and Management Schools.[32]

1. Ethical-Psychological Aims

Participation is viewed as a means of recognizing the worker as a "moral being" with certain inalienable rights to be considered as more than an inanimate factor input. It is argued, because workers have invested their labour and tied their fate to the enterprise, they have a right to influence its management and working conditions. This is essential for the development of the employee's personality as a free individual.[33] This argument has been extended by a school of psychologists and sociologists who perceive that there presently exists a basic conflict between the requirements of modern work organizations and the psychological needs of workers.[34] It is contended that the process of human maturation involves a movement from passivity to activity; from dependence to independence; from limited behaviours to multiple behaviours; from short-time perspectives to long-time perspectives; from subordinate positions to equality; and from non-awareness to self-control. However, modern industrial work organizations are generally characterized by job fragmentation, specialization and worker subordination to a hierarchial chain of controls which tend to retard the development of the worker's personality as a mature individual. Moreover, the reactions of mature workers within such organizations may be reflected in resentment, absenteeism and sabotage which are clearly detrimental to the goals of the enterprise itself. Consequently, worker participation is expected to reduce worker alienation, enhance the development of his personality, and increase job satisfaction.[35]

2. Politico-Social Aims

Frequently associated with the concept of "industrial democracy", participation is essentially seen as a means of extending the principles of democratic government to the enterprise. It has been argued, ". . . the establishment of political democracy and the theoretical equality of individual citizens in determining government policies and decisions needs to be reflected in economic or industrial democracy . . .",[36] with workers being given comparable rights to influence decisions which vitally affect them in their jobs. Moreover, traditional democratic theorists argue all men have the capacity for responsible and moral deliberation which can only be developed through participation in all institutions of the society, including the workplace. Thus, the function of participation is to educate workers in democratic skills and procedures which allow them to provide a positive contribution both to the firm and to society in general.[37] Accordingly, the specific politico-social aims of participation may include strengthened worker influence over management policies, improved terms and conditions of employment, greater integration of employees in the enterprise, and the promotion of community welfare through more democratic institutions.[38]

3. Economic Aims

Worker participation is perceived to be an effective method of utilizing human resources which, directly or indirectly, will increase enterprise efficiency and profitabilty. It is claimed, when employees are involved in the preparation of those measures and policies they are required to implement, such participation is likely to provide valuable new ideas, raise worker morale, promote a spirit of co-operation, and reduce conflict. This view of participation is primarily advocated by a growing school of management who are concerned about worker alienation as manifested in accelerating turnover, absenteeism, industrial sabotage, alcohol and drug abuse, and wildcat strikes.[39] Hence, the objective of participation is to raise productivity through reduced worker alienation, higher-quality work, new ideas on improved production techniques, greater willingness to accept necessary changes and a reduction in work stoppages.[40] It is apparent the concept of worker participation in managerial decision-making may be viewed from different perspectives and expectations. Accordingly, in order to avoid unnecessary confusion and controversy, the participants in an industrial relations system must establish clearly the particular philosophies and goals which they attribute to participation. Furthermore, the appropriate forms of participation will be influenced by these goals. To provide the concept of worker participation with more concrete meaning, a brief discussion of the prevalent forms and their respective objectives will be presented.

B. FORMS OF WORKER PARTICIPATION

A great diversity of forms of worker participation have evolved in numerous countries. These forms tend to vary according to their objectives and the requirements of the particular political-economic-social system. Specifically, the forms of participation in a given country will tend to be influenced by the structure and role of employers' organizations, the industrial relations system, the basic socio-cultural characteristics of the population, and the geographic area concerned.[41] In terms of aims and objectives, the main forms may be divided into direct and indirect participation.[42]

1. Direct Forms of Participation

Direct participation focuses on the individual employee or immediate work group and is primarily concerned with decisions related to the execution of the task. Such forms of participation include:[43]

(i) IMPROVED COMMUNICATION AND CONSUL TATION: An improved two-way flow of information and ideas between management and workers is established. Workers may be consulted on certain issues before decisions are taken.

(ii) JOB ENRICHMENT: Greater responsibility is given to the individual worker through redesign of the work organization, often increasing the variety of tasks performed, and delegation of some managerial functions. Workers may take certain decisions regarding their tasks and/or work conditions previously made for them.

(iii) SEMI-AUTONOMOUS WORK GROUPS: Work groups are granted considerable latitude in determining the organization and execution of tasks. These groups may also be given control over such matters as pace of work, ordering of raw materials and quality control.

Thus, direct forms of participation do not involve any basic change in the distribution of power between management and labour. Management still retains its unilateral decision-making powers above the level of task execution. Direct participation would appear to be consistent with ethical and economic aims where its principal functions are to improve job satisfaction and organizational performance through recognition of workers' interests and abilities.[44]

2. Indirect Forms of Participation

Indirect forms of participation involve those processes and structures whereby worker representatives influence decisions generally taken at higher organizational levels. Important forms of indirect participation include:[45]

(i)   COLLECTIVE BARGAINING: Collective bargaining rights on specified issues are granted to the union recognized as the official representative of the workers. Joint decision-making through negotiation may cover a wide range of issues, including terms and conditions of employment.

(ii) WORKS COUNCIL: Information, consultation and decision-making rights on certain matters are given to the employee representative bodies. These bodies are jointly or solely elected by the workers with possible union involvement and may provide for employer representatives. Areas of concern often involve daily management of personnel relations and welfare activities.

(iii) BOARD REPRESENTATION: Worker representatives on the enterprise's management or supervisory boards are granted the same decision-making powers on general policy issues as shareholder representatives. With the exception of West Germany, employee representatives are in a minority position.

Indirect participation may lead to a redistribution of power in favour of labour. Accordingly, it is not surprising that employers are often willing to accept direct forms of participation but are reluctant to establish indirect forms.[46] Indirect participation is consistent with politico-social aims where its basic function is to safeguard the collective interests of workers over issues not only concerning wages and working conditions but also general policy decisions such as mergers, investments, technical change, closures, expansion, lay-offs and plant relocations.[47]

Given the numerous forms of participation that can be implemented, the total amount of worker participation within an organization may be assessed according to its "scope", "degree", and "extent".[48] Scope means the range of managerial functions in which workers have the right to take part. Degree measures the extent to which workers can influence managerial decisions which may stretch from unilateral management control to unilateral worker control. The extent of participation refers to how widely it is spread among the members of the workforce. Thus, the greater the scope, degree, and extent, the greater the amount of worker participation within the enterprise.[49]

The foregoing discussion has indicated different forms of worker participation perform different functions and may be concerned with a variety of issues such as general and economic policy, employment relations, remuneration and conditions of work, and welfare activities of the enterprise.[50] Because direct and indirect forms of participation are concerned with different subject matters and objectives, they tend to be complementary and may actually reinforce their mutual success.[51] While job satisfaction is a primary concern of the worker, it is not sufficient to meet all of his growing aspirations, especially the desire to influence general policy decisions. Hence direct participation may enhance the cooperative spirit within an enterprise, but it does not recognize the need for worker representation in areas where there may be a basic conflict of interest between labour and management.[52] Bowleg has argued it would be unrealistic to expect that, ". . . management's initiative in introducing more direct participation at the immediate place of work will reduce the pressure for representative participation at the higher levels of the organization."[53] Therefore, to be operationally successful, worker participation must be allowed to meet the perceived needs of labour as well as those of management.

The Determinants of Worker Participation

In addition to considering the various objectives and potential forms of participation, attention must also be focused on the practical determinants of instituting a workable system within individual enterprises. Walker has suggested these determinants may be divided into situational and human factors.[54] The situational factors refer to certain characteristics of the firm which determine its participation potential. These characteristics include the autonomy of the enterprise, its technology, its size, and its organizational structure. The human factors refer to the workers' propensity to participate and management's acceptance of worker participation. This second set of factors determines the extent to which the participation potential of the firm is realized.

A. SITUATIONAL FACTORS

Participation potential may first be affected by the extent to which an enterprise is free to make managerial decisions. In both the private and public sectors, and in socialist and non-socialist countries, certain decisions may be taken above the enterprise level which limit the potential for worker participation. For example, in a country such as Canada, legislative provisions may be implemented which curtail decisions regarding the desired amount of participation at firm level. Moreover, multi-national enterprises may be restricted in decision-making when the formulation of company policy occurs outside the country of concern.

Second, a firm's technology may influence the potential scope, degree, extent, and form of worker participation. The more complex and specialized the technology, for example, the more knowledge is required of workers before they can effectively participate in decisions above task level. The amount of control over workers as established by technological requirements and associated administrative procedures may also influence the extent to which employees can affect working conditions and the execution of their tasks. Furthermore, the degree of worker participation may be limited if the technology and tasks cannot allow for delays while issues are discussed or negotiated. At the same time, the ability of workers to influence management decisions may also depend on the extent to which their work is essential.

A third factor determining participation potential is firm size. It is commonly observed that small firms are more readily adaptable to participative arrangements than are large firms due to greater flexibility in administrative and work procedures and more informal types of supervision. In addition, smaller firms offer more potential for direct worker involvement in decision-making above the level of the task, whereas representative participation may be the only feasible form in large establishments.

Finally, the formal organization structure of the enterprise may have an important impact on participation potential. The next chapter discusses indirect forms of worker participation, particularly board representation, which are most easily implemented in an enterprise characterized by a two-tier board structure with a clear division of responsibility between supervision and management. Moreoever, the manner in which management uses its discretion in sharing information and delegating authority of decision-making powers downwards influences the potential for participation.

Consequently, in establishing goals for increased participation, it is first necessary to examine the factors affecting the participation potential of the enterprise. It is evident that some of these factors will need to be altered, if possible, to permit the implementation of the desired participative arrangements.

B.   HUMAN FACTORS

The extent to which a firm's participation potential is realized in practice will depend on the interaction between workers' propensity to participate on the one hand, and management's willingness to accept participation on the other. Workers' propensity to participate will critically depend on their attitudes towards the general idea of influencing management decisions, the appropriate amount and forms of participation, and the degrees to which they actually wish to participate. For example, various studies have indicated that a majority of workers favour the general principle of participation and have a strong desire to influence those decisions which affect directly their own work and conditions of employment. However, only a relatively small proportion express interest in personally taking part in representative institutions concerned with the general management of the enterprise even though they support these institutions in principle.[55] Therefore, it is important to establish the proportion of the workforce holding various attitudes and also the nature and extent of differences between different groups of workers. A second factor influencing workers' propensity to participate is their capacity or ability to undertake management decisions as measured by their levels of education and training. Lastly, the workers' perceived power to influence decisions will affect their enthusiasm or apathy for participation. If workers feel they are unable to influence management decisions through their participative institutions, the result is likely to be frustration or indifference.

Management's acceptance of worker participation likewise depends on attitudes, capacities, and perceived power. The philosophy adopted by management will affect significantly the extent to which it is prepared to accept the concept of worker participation and the desired forms. Moreover, management's capacity and willingness to operate a system of worker participation will depend on the amount of training and experience held with this form of decision-making. Furthermore, manager's perception of their relative power may influence their acceptance of participation. For example, although they may have an unfavourable attitude towards participation, they may accept it if they consider the balance of power is against them.

Hence, given the participation potential of an enterprise, the amount and forms of worker participation realized in practice will be determined by the interplay between workers and management. Participative institutions must be designed to suit the attitudes and needs of the various groups within the firm, otherwise the result may be antagonism or apathy. At the same time, it should be noted that these attitudes are not static but subject to change according to economic and social changes and experience with the established forms of participation. Finally, both management and workers may require appropriate types of training in order to ensure the successful operation of these institutions for participation.

A Framework of Analysis

From the foregoing discussion it is evident that worker participation in management decision-making is a highly complex concept. Systems of participation will tend to vary among countries due to differences in political, social, and economic contexts. Moreover, the appropriate institutions may vary among industries within the same country due to the special characteristics of the organizations and the members of these organizations. Therefore, the following model may provide a useful framework for analyzing the numerous systems of participation which have evolved.[56]

```
┌─────────────────────────────────────────┐ ┐
│           EXTERNAL FACTORS              │ │
├─────────────────────────────────────────┤ │
│ Economic, political, and social context,│ │
│ legislation.                            │ │
└─────────────────────────────────────────┘ ├ DETERMINANTS
                    ↓                        │
┌─────────────────────────────────────────┐ │
│           INTERNAL FACTORS              │ │
├────────────────────┬────────────────────┤ │
│  The Participation │   Human Factors    │ │
│     Potential      │                    │ │
├────────────────────┼────────────────────┤ │
│ Technology, size,  │ Cognitive/attitudinal│ │
│ autonomy, organi-  │ characteristics of │ │
│ zation structure.  │ managers and       │ │
│                    │ workers.           │ │
└────────────────────┴────────────────────┘ ┘
                    ↓
┌─────────────────────────────────────────┐ ┐
│         FORMS AND DIMENSIONS            │ │
├─────────────────────────────────────────┤ ├ MORPHOLOGY
│ Legislated/voluntary, direct/indirect,  │ │
│ formal/informal. Degree, scope, extent, │ │
│ amount.                                 │ │
└─────────────────────────────────────────┘ ┘
                    ↓
┌─────────────────────────────────────────┐ ┐
│           INTERNAL EFFECTS              │ │
├─────────────────────────────────────────┤ │
│ Changes in productivity, absenteeism,   │ │
│ turnover, conflict, motivation, satisfac-│ │
│ tion, work attitudes, health and safety,│ │
│ self-actualization, working conditions, │ │
│ decision-making powers.                 │ │
└─────────────────────────────────────────┘ ├ CONSEQUENCES
                    ↓                        │
┌─────────────────────────────────────────┐ │
│           EXTERNAL EFFECTS              │ │
├─────────────────────────────────────────┤ │
│ Impact on public opinion; democratization│ │
│ of society at large; pressure for further│ │
│ legislation.                            │ │
└─────────────────────────────────────────┘ ┘
```

Using this framework of analysis, the determinants of participation consist of factors both external and internal to the enterprise. The "morphology" of participation refers to its dimensions (whether the institutions are established through legislation or voluntary agreement and whether the arrangements are formal or informal), the forms it may take, and the actual amount of participation. The consequences of participation include the impact of the enterprise itself, such as changes in productivity, worker satisfaction, working conditions, and the distribution of power between labour and management, as well as its impact on society as a whole, which may involve the development of more democratic institutions.

The following chapter describes several important systems of worker participation which are currently operating or being proposed in Western Europe.

Notes

[1] Franz, V.R.W., Holloway, R.G., and Lonergan, W.G. *The Organization Survey Feedback Principle as a Technique for Encouraging Workers' Involvement in Organization Improvement*. Geneva, International Institute for Labour Studies, 1970, p.2.

[2] Secretariat, OECD, *Work in a Changing Industrial Society*. Paris, OECD, 1974, p.5.

[3] Dufty, N.F. *Changes in Labour-Management Relations in the Enterprise*. Paris, OECD, 1975, pp. 76-96. Dufty's model is a modification of A.W.J. Craig's input-output model of an industrial relations system.

[4] The environment also contains ecological and political subsystems: however, they are not seen as primary causes of change in an industrial relations system. See Dufty, *op. cit.*, pp.77 and 79.

[5] Franz, Holloway and Lonergan of the University of Chicago Industrial Relations Center would disagree with this approach stating, ". . . theory based on historical, economic, political, organizational and industrial relations assumptions seems to be an inadequate frame of reference in which to account for the worker participation phenomena." They have adopted a more sociological approach, termed the "rational-social/psychological-behavioural" or "SPMOD" system. See Franz, Holloway, Lonergan, *op. cit.*, pp. 10-11; 18.

6 Dufty, *op. cit.*, p.80.

7 Daniel, W.W., "Report on the discussion at the Seminar," *Prospects for Labour/Management Co-operation in the Enterprise*, Paris, OECD, 1974, pp.19-20.

8 Bowleg, J.T., "Final report on the Seminar," *Workers' Participation*, Paris, OECD, 1975, p.72: Daniel, *op. cit.*, , p.20.

9 Barbash, J., "Final Report on the Conference," *Work in a Changing Industrial Society*, Paris, OECD., 1974, pp.26-27.

10 K. Newton has illustrated that the number of pair relations among members of an organization will tend to increase exponentially with the size of the organization, thus implying that these costs of labour aggregation will be multiplied for large establishments. See K. Newton, *The Theory and Practice of Industrial Democracy: A Canadian Perspective*, Discussion Paper No. 94, Ottawa, Economic Council of Canada, 1977.

11 Dufty, *op. cit.*, pp.80, 82-97.

12 Bowleg, *op. cit.*, p.32; Dufty, *op. cit.*, p.82; Daniel, *op. cit.*, p.5.

13 Dufty, *op. cit.*, ., p.84.

14 Chotard, Y., "Statement," *Workers' Participation*, Paris, OECD, 1975, p.14.

15 K.O. Alexander, "On Work and Authority: Issues in Job Enlargement, Job Enrichment, Worker Participation, and Shared Authority," *American Journal of Economics and Sociology*, vol. 34, No.1, January 1975, p.45; Garnett, J., *Practical Policies for Participation*, London, The Industrial Society, 1974, p.6.

16 Dufty, *op. cit.*, pp.84 and 85.

17 Dufty, *op. cit.*, p.86; Daniel, *op. cit.*, ., p.20.

18 Shutt, II., ed., *Worker Participation in West Germany, Sweden, Yugoslavia, and the United Kingdom*, London, The Economist Intelligence Unit, 1975, p.1.

19 Daniel, *op. cit.*, p.13.

20 Dufty, *op. cit.*, p.89.

21 This is particularly evident in the United Kingdom and Western Europe where unions are demanding parity representation on supervisory boards.

22 Sturmthal, A.F., *Workers' Participation in Management: A Review of United States Experience*, Geneva, International Institute for Labour Studies, 1970, p.184.

23 Dufty, *op. cit.*, p. 90.

24 L.E. Preston and J.E. Post, "The Third Managerial Revolution," *Academy of Management Journal*, Vol. 17, No. 3, September 1974, p.476; Newton, *op. cit.*, p.5.

25 Dufty, *op. cit.*, p.90. This view has been well articulated by two employer representatives who stated: "Greater participation gives support for authority: decisions are more readily accepted if they are understood. . ." but ". . .in order to preserve and even develop the essential aspects of the enterprise's efficiency. . . the hands of those who have to take the responsibility and consequences of decisions must at all costs be kept free." Chotard, *op. cit.*, p.20; Decosterd, R., "Concluding Remarks," *Workers' Participation*, p.29.

²⁶ Dufty, *op. cit.,* p.91. Dufty points out that the range of issues normally covered by today's collective agreements would be inconceivable to 19th century managers.

²⁷ Dufty, *op. cit.,* p.91; Preston and Post, *op. cit.,* p.477; Newton, *op. cit.,* p.5.

²⁸ Bowleg, *op. cit.,* p.52; Daniel, *op. cit.,* p.11; Barbash, *op. cit.,* p.18.

²⁹ Andras, R.K., "Introductory Speech," *Work in a Changing Industrial Society,* Paris, OECD, 1975, p.12

³⁰ CIR, *Worker Participation and Collective Bargaining in Europe,* London, Her Majesty's Stationery Office, 1974, p.3.

³¹ International Labour Organization, *Participation of Workers in Decisions Within Undertakings,* Labour-Management Series: No. 33, Geneva, International Labour Office, 1969, pp.6-12; Walker, K.F., "The Concept and Its Implementation," *Workers' Participation in Management,* Geneva, International Institute for Labour Studies, 1967, pp.14-17.

³² Greenberg's fourth school of thought, termed the Participatory Left, is not considered in this paper as it is based on the aim of raising worker consciousness for the ultimate objective of establishing socialism. It is felt that this aim would not be acceptable, and hence not applicable, within the Canadian context. See Greenberg, E.S., "The Consequences of Worker Participation: A Clarification of the Theroretical Literature," *Social Science Quarterly,* Vol. 56, No. 52, September 1975, pp.190-209.

³³ International Labour Organization, *Workers Participation in Decisions Within Undertakings,* Labour-Management Series: No. 48, Geneva, International Labour Office, 1974, p. 65; Walker, *op. cit.,* p. 15; ILO, 1969, *op. cit.,* p.7.

³⁴ Greenberg, *op. cit.,* pp.194-197; Newton, *op. cit.,* p.10.

³⁵ Walker, K.F., *Worker's Participation in Management, An International Perspective,* Geneva, International Institute for Labour Studies, 1972, p.1177.

³⁶ Shutt, *op. cit.,* p.3.

³⁷ Greenberg, *op. cit.,* pp.179-200; Newton, *op. cit.,* p.11.

³⁸ ILO, 1969, *op. cit.,* pp.9-10, 137; Walker, 1972, *op. cit.,.,* p.1177.

³⁹ Greenberg, *op. Cit.,* pp.192-194; Newton, *op. cit.,* p.9.

⁴⁰ ILO, 1969, *op. cit.,* p.11-147; Walker, 1967, *op. cit.,* p.15; Walker, 1967, *op. cit.,* p.1177.

⁴¹ ILO, 1969, *op. cit.,* p. 138.

⁴² Bowleg, *op. cit.,* pp. 35-37.

⁴³ Bowleg, *op. cit.,* p.35; Shutt, *op. cit.,* pp.2-3.

⁴⁴ Bowleg, *op. cit.,* p.36; Shutt, *op. cit.,* p.2.

⁴⁵ Bowleg, *op. cit.,* p.36; Shutt, *op. cit.,* pp.2-3; ILO, *op. cit.,* pp.139-140.

⁴⁶ Bowleg, *op. cit.,* pp.42-43.

⁴⁷ Bowleg, *op. cit.,* pp.36-37.

⁴⁸ Newton, *op. cit.,* p.20

[49] Kwoka has proposed the following equation which theoretically could be used to quantify the amount of participation in an organization:

$$P = \sum_{i=1}^{n} S_i d(S_i)$$

where P is a single number measuring the amount of participation, S_i are the levels of scope which are numbered from 1 to n according to the importance of the management function, and $d(S_i)$ are the degrees of participation in that function, ranging from 0 for no worker control to 5 for unilateral worker control. See Kwoka, J.E. Jr., "The Organization of Work: A Conceptual Framework," *Social Science Quarterly,* Vol. 57, No. 3, 1976, pp.632-643.

[50] ILO, 1969, *op. cit.,* pp.141-152.

[51] Bowleg, *op. cit.,* pp. 42-43; Shutt, *op. cit.,* pp.3-5.

[52] Shutt, *op. cit.,* p.4.

[53] Bowleg, *op. cit.,* p.43.

[54] Walker, 1972, *op. cit.,* pp.1176-1183; see also Newton, *op. cit.,* pp.27-30.

[55] See Walker, *op. cit.,* p.1181.

[56] This framework is adapted from Newton's "An Organization - Theoretic Framework for Analysis of Participation." Newton, *op. cit.,* p.35.

II

Worker Participation in Western Europe

Worker participation has received greatest attention in Western Europe where virtually every country has adopted or is planning to adopt some formal means of extending worker influence over company management. This chapter describes four of the more significant models: the West German model, currently the most sophisticated and successful system of worker participation; the Dutch model, an important variation of the West German plan; the EEC Commission proposals for a common framework to be adopted by the European Community; and the United Kingdom proposals for a system of worker participation which could be integrated into their highly developed collective bargaining context.

I. The West German Model

Although worker participation in Germany first found legal expression in the Works Councils Law of 1920[1], a comprehensive system was not instituted until the period following the Second World War. In fact, the present West German industrial relations system evolved from the post-war reconstruction period. At this time, the trade unions established a unified organization and a system of extensive worker participation in industry for the purpose of preventing any future destruction of their organization or the re-emergence of a corporate state and misuse of economic power.[2] The trade unions also adopted a philosophy of responsibility and co-partnership with management for ensuring the success of the West German socio-economic system. This attitude has led the trade unions to press for an extension of co-determination powers within West German enterprises.[3]

A. COLLECTIVE BARGAINING

1. The Trade Unions
The West German constitution guarantees both the right of the individual to belong to a trade union and the right of the trade union to develop freely.[4] Following the Second World War, unions were re-established on an industry basis where the employees in a particular industrial sector are organized under one union. The present rate of unionization is approximately thirty percent although the figures for certain large industries range from seventy to one hundred per cent.[5]

The Federation of German Trade Unions (DGB) constitutes the principal central union organization where it is comprised of sixteen industrial unions representing eighty per cent of total unionized labour.[6] Its general functions are to represent members' interests in matters relating to legislation and social policy and to co-ordinate members' collective bargaining activities. The actual bargaining process is the responsibility of the individual trade unions. The DGB provides substantial information to members for collective bargaining purposes through its institute of economic and social research. In addition, the union movement is closely involved in the political process where an estimated seventy per cent of total unionized workers are active members of a political party.[7] Furthermore, the Federation has strengthened its influence on the economy by establishing certain business ventures which include a bank with branches in most major German cities, one of the largest construction companies in Germany, and a large insurance holding company.[8] It has been argued this close identification with the country's political and economic system has engendered a responsible and co-operative union attitude in collective bargaining.[9]

2. The Employers
The main representative organization for management is the Federal Association of German Employers (BDA) whose membership comprises eight hundred associations representing eighty per cent of German employers,[10] Like the DGB, its primary functions are to co-ordinate members' negotiation activities and influence legislation. The Association also provides members with economic information and advice on personnel matters. It should be noted the BDA strongly supports consultative forms of worker participation but has resisted union demands for extension of co-determination rights. On the basis

of this ideology, the BDA excluded employers in the coal, iron and steel industries from membership as their companies engage in parity representation on supervisory boards.[11]

3. The Government

The West German government has provided a number of institutions to encourage labour-management co-operation.[12] Social insurance schemes are administered by self-governing public corporations consisting of equal numbers of employee and employer representatives. The DGB and BDA participate in the management of the Federal Insurance Institute for Salaried Employees and the Advisory Board for Pension Claims. In addition, both federations recommend appointments to the Labour Courts[13] and participate in the collective bargaining committee of the Federal Labour Ministry.[14] Moreover, the federal government has initiated two noteworthy programs intended to provide current information concerning the operation of the economy.[15] Under the "Concerted Action Program", every three months the Minister of Finance conducts a meeting with representatives from all groups having a direct effect on the economy, including unions, management, banks, commercial institutions and government. The purpose of these discussions is to allow each group to present their views on the state of the economy. The participants are then expected to use this information in their subsequent collective bargaining, pricing or interest rate setting activities.[16] A second source of information is the Council of Economic Advisors which consists of five academic economists who additionally review the state of the economy and issue periodic forecasts. It has been observed that these two programs often serve as important reference points for labour and management prior to negotiations, tending to moderate union expectations and bargaining policies.[17]

4. Collective Agreements

Collective agreements are normally concluded for an industry in a particular region.[18] These agreements are legally binding on the employees and employers who accede to them. Bargainable issues generally concern wages, terms and conditions of employment and may include such issues as technological change. Wage settlements are the minimum rates which must be paid by the companies to the agreement; however, individual enterprises may offer higher wages if they desire.[19]

The Works Constitution Act ensures that the responsibility and tasks of the trade unions in collective bargaining are not affected by the provisions for worker participation within the individual enterprise. Under the Act, collective agreements take precedence over agreements concluded with the works councils. Therefore, it has been argued, by regulating co-operation between the trade unions and works councils, the Works Constitution Act strengthens trade union influence at the establishment level.[20]

B. THE WORKS COUNCIL

1. General Principles

German works councils are governed by the Works Constitution Act of 1972.[21] The Act supports the principle of co-operation between the employer and works council in compliance with the collective agreements in force and with the representative trade unions and employers' associations for the benefit of the employees and of the establishment.[22] Industrial disputes between the employer and works council are prohibited. Differences of opinion are to be settled either through a decision of an arbitration board composed of an equal number of employer and employee representatives and an independent chairman.

The Works Constitution Act also grants trade unions certain rights within the establishment. Trade unions have the right to participate in the quarterly plant-wide council meetings, to attend other council meetings if this is desired by one quarter of the works council members, and access to the establishment for the purpose of exercising their designated rights and function.[23] Moreover, even though trade unions are not entitled to submit a list of candidates in works council elections, estimates are that over eighty per cent of present council members belong to unions.[24]

2. Establishment and Composition of the Works Council

Works councils are to be instituted in every industrial establishment with five or more employees. The council consists entirely of worker representatives who are elected through secret ballot *by all employees entitled to vote*. Employees eighteen years of age or over are entitled to vote and any employee, excluding supervisory staff, who has reached eighteen and has been employed by the enterprise for at least six months is eligible for election. The size of the works council is determined by the number of persons employed by the establishment where the number ranges from one representative in plants with five to twenty workers to thirty-five or more in plants with over nine thousand workers.[25] Council members are to serve a three-year term. In establishments employing more than twenty workers, provision is made for proportional representation of workers and salaried employees. Furthermore, a central works council is to be set up in those enterprises with several establishments. The central works council, normally composed of two representatives from each establishment works council, is responsible for matters concerning the enterprise as a whole or several of its establishments. Finally, in a group of companies, a group works council may be established by majority decision of the central works councils of the individual companies in the group.[26]

Works council members are given special protection and facilities to ensure their independence and efficient operation. A member cannot be dismissed from employment while holding office or for one year thereafter unless otherwise approved by the works council or decided by the Labour Court. The employer must incur all costs arising from the council's activities as well as provide necessary materials, office staff, and premises. Members must be released from their regular employment obligations, without loss of pay, to the extent necessary for the performance of their duties as councillors. In addition, establishments employing more than three hundred workers are required to allow a certain number of employee representatives (determined by the size of the establishment) to act as full-time council members. Moreover, during their term of office, members may obtain a total of three weeks paid leave from work to participate in educational and training courses pertaining to works council activities.[27]

Works council meetings are usually held once a month during regular working hours. The employer or his representatives may only attend those meeting initiated by him or through invitation of the works council. The council submits a progress report of its activities to the quarterly meeting of all employees and the employer. This meeting can neither dissolve the works council nor remove individual members. Such action is only possible by a decision of the Labour Court when it is applied for by one quarter of the employees or a representative trade union on the grounds that the council or individual members have infringed statutory obligations.[28]

3. Rights and Functions

The general obligations of the works council include handling employee grievances within the establishment, ensuring the interests of different employee groups are respected and effect is given to acts, ordinances, safety regulations, collective agreements and works agreements for the benefit of the workers.[29] The works council has participation rights ranging from the receipt of information to co-decision in specified social, personnel and economic matters.[30]

The works council has co-determination rights concerning: organization of the establishment, hours of work, holiday arrangements, technical installations to measure worker productivity, social facilities, administration of company-owned housing, wage structure and rates of pay, piecework and bonus plans, health and safety regulations, and the implementation of training schemes in the establishment. The council also has rights to information and consultation regarding the structure, organization and design of jobs, work flow, work environment and vocational training. If workers are significantly affected by changes in these areas, the council can request that appropriate measures be taken to protect their interests. Where there are differences of opinion between the employer and works council, the arbitration board can provide a binding decision.

Certain matters affecting staff within the establishment, such as recruitment, job grading, regrading, the transfer, promotion or dismissal of employees, require works council approval. If the employer wishes to undertake such matters despite works council opposition, he must normally appeal to the Labour Court. In addition, a worker dismissed without prior consent to the council may appeal to the Labour Court where the dismissal becomes void if the appeal is upheld.

The Works Constitution Act maintains the principle of employer responsibility for economic decisions. However, the works council has been granted substantial information and consultation rights over such issues. The council may establish an economic committee in companies employing more than one hundred workers for the purpose of discussing economic matters with management. The works council and committee are entitled to information on the economic and financial situation of the enterprise, production, marketing and investment programs. Furthermore, the employer must inform and consult the works council regarding any proposed changes in the establishment which could adversely affect its employees. Such changes would encompass: the contraction, closure or transfer of the establishment or substantial parts of it, mergers, fundamental changes in the organization or objectives of the company, and the introduction of new work and manufacturing methods. The employer and works council are expected to attempt to reach a compromise over the proposed change which considers the interests of all concerned groups within the enterprise as well as developing a social plan designed to minimize any resulting economic disadvantages suffered by the employees. While the employer has the right of final decision regarding such changes, the works council has co-decision rights over the social plan. If the works council and employer cannot agree on the context of the social plan, the decision of the arbitration board is binding. In its decision, the arbitration board must take into account both the interests of the affected employees and the economic situation of the enterprise.

It would appear that both German Management and labour consider the works council system of worker participation to be generally successful in fulfilling its specified functions.[31] Works councils are seen as the primary means of involving all employees in the decision-making process at establishment level. At the same time, it should be regarded as distinct from and complementary to worker participation at board level.

C. WORKER PARTICIPATION AT BOARD LEVEL

1. Company Structure

Most German enterprises are controlled by means of a formal two-tier board structure, consisting of a supervisory and a management board.[32] Members of the supervisory board are elected by the shareholders' general meeting or appointed by certain shareholders or a class of shareholders. The number of members may range from a minimum of three to a maximum of twenty-one, depending on the size of the enterprise. The management board contains one or more members who are appointed by the supervisory board and may serve a maximum term of five years. The supervisory board may also appoint a member of the management board to be chairman. An individual may not be simultaneously a member of both boards.[33]

German company law establishes a clear division of function and responsibility between the two boards.[34] The supervisory board is responsible for major policy decisions concerning the enterprise and for regulating the management board. The management board is responsible for the daily administration of the company and has specific obligations for reporting the company's affairs to the supervisory board. Management is required to provide a continuous flow of information to the supervisory board regarding the current state of the enterprise and proposed management policy. In addition, the supervisory board is entitled to investigate the company's affairs through an inspection of its books and records and may require management to provide specific reports or answer detailed questions. Although the supervisory board cannot acquire managerial functions, it may specify that certain management plans receive its prior consent. If consent is not obtained, the management board can only proceed with the plan if it receives a three-quarters majority vote at a shareholders' meeting.

It has been argued that the two-tier system is probably the best structure for providing worker participation at board level.[35] By separating the supervisory and managerial by functions, this structure allows for the representation of diverse interests on the supervisory board while maintaining an effective homogeneous management body.

2.   The Coal, Iron and Steel Industries

The Co-determination Act of 1951 established a system of parity representation between shareholders and employees on the supervisory boards of companies in the coal, iron and steel industries.[36] This Act applies to all companies in these industries employing more than one thousand workers. The supervisory board is normally composed of eleven members, five of which are nominated by the employees, five by the shareholders and the eleventh ''independent'' member is co-opted. Two of the employee representatives are to be workers nominated by the works council, and three are to be nominated by trade unions represented in the company where one candidate must be independent of the employees and trade unions. Four of the shareholder representatives are to be appointed by the general meeting without restriction while the fifth appointment must be independent of the shareholders and employees. The shareholder and employee representatives then nominate a neutral eleventh member. Worker representatives have the same rights and responsibilities as the shareholder representatives and are required to maintain confidentiality of information.[37]

The management board must include an Employees' Director responsible for industrial relations, personnel and social matters. This member cannot be appointed or dismissed without the majority approval of the employee representatives on the supervisory board.

3.   Other Industries

Prior to 1975, the Works Constitution Act required a minimum of one-third worker representation on supervisory boards of companies outside the mining and steel industries if they employed more than five hundred workers. Under the Act, the employee nominees were elected through ballot by all workers in the enterprise. Employees and the works councils could submit candidate lists, but not the trade unions.[38]

Mainly as the result of continued pressure by trade unions and the Social Democratic Party, a new model extending employee representation was established in 1975.[39] This model applies to all enterprises outside the mining and steel industries employing more than two thousand workers. The supervisory board is composed of ten workers' and ten shareholders' representatives. Of the worker representatives, six are to be nominated by all workers in the enterprise, three by the trade unions and one by the white collar or supervisory employees. The chairman is to be co-opted by the board unless a two-thirds majority cannot be obtained, whereupon the appointment rests with the shareholders' representatives. Resolutions are to be carried by simple majority; however, shareholders have the right to veto any issue which they consider essential to their interests. Finally, all members of the management board are to be elected by majority decision, thus eliminating worker representatives' veto power over the appointment of the Employees' Director. If the supervisory board cannot agree on the appointment of the management board, final decision will lie with the shareholders' general meeting.

It should be noted this new model is a compromise arising out of the various proposals put forward by the trade unions, employer associations and political parties. Yet it has apparently not met with any general acceptance. The employer associations have argued the new system will likely impede efficient decision-making and allow the trade unions to become too dominant, which in turn may endanger the success of the free enterprise system. The Federation of German Trade Unions have argued the system is not as effective in representing workers' interests as that operating in the mining and steel industries. They are particularly suspicious of the white collar representative whom they feel is more likely to identify with shareholders' interests.[40] Consequently, there seems to be a basic disagreement between labour and management concerning the appropriate extent of worker participation on company boards. While German employers have generally accepted minority worker representation as an important means of promoting an attitude of responsibility and co-operation necessary for the efficient operation of the enterprise, they have continually rejected extension of principle of co-determination. On the other hand, the trade unions view extended co-determination as essential for pursuing their philosophy of equal partnership with management.[41] As the new model has only recently been instituted, its relative success and acceptability remains to be seen.

II. The Dutch Model

Before the Second World War, worker participation in the Netherlands involved mainly industry-wide collective bargaining as trade unions attempted to gain recognition and improve their members' working conditions. However, an attitude of co-operation between labour and management developed due to their close contact during the War and the subsequent reconstruction period. At this time various formal bodies were established at the national and industry level for purposes of consultation and co-operation.[42]

A. COLLECTIVE BARGAINING

1. The Trade Unions

As in the case of West Germany, Dutch trade unions are organized primarily on an industrial basis and represent approximately thirty-five per cent of the working population.[43] However, the trade union movement tends to be divided along religious and ideological lines where three main federations, representing about eighty per cent of total unionized workers, are identified. These are the Netherlands Federation of Trade Unions (NVV), the Christian National Trade Union Federation (CNV), and the Netherlands Catholic Trade Union Federation (NKV).[44] Unlike the West German DGB, these federations are responsible for negotiations over certain crucial issues such as wages. Individual industrial unions are given the role of implementing centrally-determined policies and may negotiate with the relevant employer associations in the name of their federation.[45]

As a result of this centralized structure, there is relatively little union involvement at the establishment level, although recently individual unions have been attempting to secure greater influence and member contact in the plant. A growing number of unions are providing a "company worker", who is a full-time union employee, to act as a link between district union officials and union members within the enterprise. Unionized workers elect a committee from among their members; the chairman of this group then liaises with the "company worker" and reports back to the committee. The committee generally deals with such matters as worker grievances and problems, and in some cases may elect their own delegation to conduct negotiations with plant management concerning the application of the centrally-determined collective agreement. However, enterprise bargaining is still fairly common.[46]

2. The Employers

Employer associations also tend to be affiliated on religious or ideological bases. The two principal representative organizations are the Association of Netherlands Enterprises (VNO) and the Federation of Catholic and Protestant Employers Association (FCWV). These bodies are responsible for negotiating with the union federations as well as for joint formulation and administration of national economic and social policy. In addition, industry associations may negotiate for their members at the industry level.[47]

3. The Government

In terms of encouraging labour-management co-operation, the most significant government institution is the Social and Economic Council (SER) which was established under the 1950 Industrial Organization Act. This forty-five member body contains equal numbers of representatives from the central employer and union organizations and independent experts. Its primary function is to advise the government on major social and economic matters as well as publish a semi-annual economic report. The SER has become highly influential in government policy where legislation is normally drafted only after agreement has been reached through extensive consultation with the Council.[48] In 1971, the SER introduced a Merger Code which is seen to be a noteworthy provision for labour-management consultation at the enterprise level. The Code requires trade unions to be informed and consulted in advance of company mergers. Management must disclose the reasons for the merger and its potential social and economic consequences. Union-management consultations should consider the social policy to be pursued after the merger.[49]

4. Collective Agreements

Dutch legislation establishes that collective agreements are legally binding and can be concluded at the national, industry or enterprise level. In addition, these agreements may be extended by legislation to cover firms not represented in negotiations. Bargainable issues may include remuneration, hours, holidays and other terms and conditions of employment. Similar to the West German system, collective agreements take precedence over agreements reached with the works councils. In practice, collective agreements are usually concluded at the national level, consequently a large proportion of employees tend to be covered by a small number of agreements. Yet, recently there has been a trend towards decentralized bargaining within particular industrial sectors or single large enterprises, for example, in the metal, chemical and construction industries.[50]

B. THE WORKS COUNCIL

1. General Principles

Dutch works councils were legally established by the Works Councils Act of 1950 and are presently regulated by the 1971 amendment which extended considerably their functions and powers. Under the 1950 Act, works councils were based on the principle of promoting co-operation and a community of interest through consultation between the employer and worker representatives. The 1971 Act maintains the original principle of co-operation but emphasizes that the council, ". . . is not only a consultative body but also represents the workers and defends their specific interests".[51] The 1971 Act further provides for substantial trade union involvement in the works council, including the right of the council to call in trade union experts for the purpose of allowing the council to function more effectively and independently.[52]

2. Establishment and Composition of Works Council

The 1971 Act requires works councils to be established in all companies employing a minimum of one hundred workers. A central works council may be created in those enterprises having more than one plant if a majority of the individual councils so desire. The central works council is to be responsible for matters common to all establishments. In addition, a group-level enterprise council may be set up which is responsible for a specific activity of the group. Finally, works councils are authorized to appoint committees, comprised of council members, for the purpose of dealing with matters affecting particular groups of workers, such as young or foreign employees.[53]

With the exception of the chief executive of the enterprise acting as chairman, works council members are elected by the employees. All workers who have reached the age of twenty-one and have been employed by the firm for at least one year are entitled to vote while those with a minimum of three years service may be candidates for election. Candidate lists may be submitted by trade unions represented in the establishment and by non-union employees, provided their list is supported by one-third of the workers with voting rights. Members of the works council serve a two-year term and may seek re-election. As with German works councils, establishment size determines the number of council members which may range from a minimum of three to a maximum of twenty-five in firms with six thousand or more employees.

Works council members enjoy special rights similar to those of their German counterparts. These rights include protection from dismissal for two years after holding office unless otherwise ruled by courts of law, employer assumption of all costs arising from council activities, and entitlement to be absent for a given number of days each year (to be determined by the council) at full pay for educational and training purposes. Moreover, the council or chairman may call in experts, such as union leaders or specialists, for discussing special subjects.

The works council must hold a minimum of six meetings per year where two allow for a discussion with supervisory board members on the general progress of activities of the enterprise. At least once a year the employer must provide information on recruitment, remuneration, training, promotion and dismissal policy for discussion. Finally, the works council submits an annual report and reports on its meeting to all employees.[54]

3. Rights and Functions

Although they tend to be more limited, the rights and functions of the Dutch works council are similar to those provided under the German system. The council is entitled to information, consultation or co-decision rights on specific social, personnel and economic matters unless these are already covered by a collective agreement.[55]

Under the 1971 Act, the employer must receive the prior opinion of the works council on decisions concerning: wage structure and rates of pay, training and welfare schemes, and staff assessment systems. In addition, the council has co-decision rights over work rules, pension, profit sharing and savings schemes, working hours and holidays, safety, health and hygiene measures. If the employer and works council cannot reach agreement, the issue may be decided by an industry committee created by the SER which is composed of labour and management representatives.

The council has information rights regarding employer policy on remuneration, training, recruitment, promotion and dismissal. Furthermore, the employer must obtain the prior opinion of the council before implementing any changes in recruitment, promotion or dismissal policy.

The council is entitled to receive information concerning the economic position of the firm, including the annual accounts and distribution of profits. Council members are obliged to maintain confidentiality on those matters specified by the chairman or the council itself. Moreover, the employer may withhold certain vital information if it is considered necessary for the protection of the enterprise or of persons directly involved in its affairs. Finally, unless major interests are involved, prior consultation is required on decisions pertaining to contraction, expansion, closure or transfer of control of the enterprise or substantial parts of it, important organizational changes, change in location, and commencement or termination of permanent co-operation between the enterprise and other enterprises.

It would appear that both labour and management advocate the development of works councils as an essential means of allowing for worker participation in managerial decision-making.[56] However, there seems to be considerable disagreement over the proper role and function of the council. Employers tend to support the works council primarily as an advisory body and oppose co-decision, particularly through trade union machinery.[57] The trade union movement has generally pressed for extended council powers but the federations seem to disagree on which powers are to be extended and the appropriate council structure. While the CNV has argued for wider co-decision rights on social policy issues and maintaining the present council structure, the NVV has argued for veto rights over important economic matters and the removal of the management representative as chairman.[58]

C. WORKER PARTICIPATION AT BOARD LEVEL

1. Company Structure
The 1971 Netherlands Act[59] pertaining to company reorganization has established a formal two-tier system similar to that existing in West Germany. Under this Act, all public and private limited companies with minimum capital assets of ten million guilders, having a works council, or employing at least one hundred workers in the Netherlands must create a supervisory and management board. The supervisory board, containing at least three members who serve a four-year term, is initially appointed by the shareholders' general meeting. New members are then appointed through co-option between the shareholders and employees. Members of the management board are appointed and dismissed by the supervisory board after notification has been given to the general meeting of shareholders and the works council.

Division of function and responsibility between the two boards is analogous to the West German system. The management board, under the control of the supervisory board, is responsible for managing the company's business and informing the supervisory board of its affairs. It must likewise obtain the supervisory board's consent before implementing major decisions affecting the enterprise. The supervisory board is also responsible for settling annual accounts, subject to the approval of the shareholders' general meeting.[60]

Those companies not covered by the 1971 Act are subject to the Company Act of 1928. This act additionally provides for a two-tier structure where both the supervisory and management board are appointed by the general shareholders' meeting. Moreover, these companies may voluntarily adopt the new provisions of the 1971 Act. Therefore, most large and medium-sized Dutch companies have had a fairly long tradition of two-tier board structures.[61]

2. The Co-option System

Employees are now entitled to participate in the appointment of supervisory board members in companies covered by the 1971 Act. The Act specifies new board members are to be appointed by co-option of existing members. However, the shareholders' meeting, works council or central works council, and management board may nominate candidates for appointment subject to the restriction that the candidates are not in the service of the company or its subsidiaries, or trade union members involved in negotiations with the company. Furthermore, the works council and shareholders' meeting may veto a candidate proposed by the supervisory board if it is believed this person is unsuitable as a member or his appointment would alter the appropriate composition of the board. The supervisory board may appeal the veto to the Social and Economic Council where the final decision will lie with a Council committee after consultations with all concerned parties.[62]

This alternative approach to worker participation at the supervisory board level was proposed by the SER in 1969 in a unanimous report. Its stated purpose, ". . . is to ensure that the board of directors enjoys the confidence both of the shareholders and of the workers."[63] The Council feels the co-option system is preferable to direct employee representation as it reduces the possibility of member polarization and faction while at the same time providing workers with an equal opportunity to influence the composition of the board.[64] Moreover, it eliminates the problem of worker directors being faced with a loyalty conflict in attempting to serve both the interests of the enterprise and the employees. While employers probably unanimously support consultation and co-option over direct worker participation, there appears to be no general agreement on the appropriate system within the trade union movement.[65] As the system has been in operation only since 1973, experience with its effectiveness is still limited.

III. The European Economic Community Proposals

While the EEC Commission recognizes there are, ". . . real divergences in existing systems deriving from variations in the evolution of the social and economic histories of the Member States'',[66] it has put forward two proposals for a common company framework which have significant implications for worker participation in the Community. These proposals are the European Companies Statute and the Draft Fifth Directive. First proposed in 1970, the European Companies Statute is designed to facilitate the operation of a "European" Market by creating "European" enterprises subject to a standard company law. Accordingly, the provisions of the Statute are aimed at enterprises wishing to undertake a merger, the establishment of a joint holding company or joint subsidiaries across national boundaries. The 1972 Draft Fifth Directive is intended to establish a common legal structure for all public companies in the EEC. While the statute would only apply to those companies which choose to adopt its provisions, the Directive would be of general application within the European Community, where its effect would be given through appropriate national legislation.[67]

A. THE EUROPEAN COMPANIES STATUTE

In terms of employee participation, the Statute contains specific provisions for worker directors and works councils within the European Community.[68]

1. Company Structure and Worker Directors
The Statute requires the establishment of the two-tier board structure where at least one-third of the supervisory board members will be worker representatives elected by national employee organizations.[69]

Depending on the size of the enterprise, a minimum of one worker representative must NOT be employed by the firm. All supervisory board members have identical rights and obligations.

The division of function and responsibility between the two boards is very similar to the West German and Dutch systems. The supervisory board regulates and appoints the management board, including the chairman and personnel representative. The management board is required to provide the supervisory board with draft accounts, quarterly progress reports, communications on all matters of importance, and any other requested information such as special reports or documents. In addition, the supervisory board must authorize all decisions concerning mergers, closure or transfer of the enterprise or substantial parts of it, significant reductions or extensions of its activities, and important organizational changes. Finally, two clauses of the Statute enable the supervisory board to engage in collective bargaining with trade unions represented in its establishments. These European collective agreements would be binding on all employees who are members of the unions.

2. The Works Council

A European works council is to be created for companies with establishments in more than one member-country and a group works council is required for a European company with subsidiaries. National provisions for works councils are recognized as additional bodies. To accommodate differing member practices, council size and election procedures are subject to individual national legislation.

Works council members are entitled to all facilities necessary for the performance of their duties and protection against dismissal. In order to effectively discharge their functions, the council is granted co-decision, consultation and information rights on certain matters. Co-decision rights include the determination of rules on recruitment, promotion and dismissal, safety, health and hygiene, the implementation of vocational training, the introduction of social facilities, terms of remuneration and the introduction of new payment methods, hours of work, and holiday schedules. If agreement cannot be reached between the works council and management, the issue may be submitted to an Arbitration Court. The works council is to give its prior opinion on management decisions concerning the operation of job evaluation schemes and the payment system. Furthermore, the supervisory board must consult the council before arriving at a decision on the above four issues requiring its authorization. If the council considers the decision will adversely affect the employees' interests, provision is made for the negotiation or settlement by arbitration of the issue. Finally, information rights include a minimum of four meetings per year with the management board and a quarterly report containing the economic position of the company, investments, and any development which may have an appreciable effect on the interests of the employees.

B.   THE DRAFT FIFTH DIRECTIVE

The Directive is the fifth of a series concerned with creating a common framework of company law within the EEC. It is particulary significant for its intention to establish worker participation at supervisory board level on a community-wide basis. It does not consider the issue of works councils, perhaps because most member countries had national provisions at the time the Directive was released.

Under the Directive, all public companies are to have supervisóry boards, but employee representation is only required for those enterprises employing more than five hundred workers. Worker representation on the supervisory board may be attained in one of two ways:

(i)   on the basis of the old German model where at least one-third of the members are appointed through nomination by the workers or their representatives;

(ii)   on the basis of the Dutch model where all board members are co-opted subject to the approval of the worker representatives and general shareholders' meeting.

The respective functions and responsibilities of the supervisory and management boards are comparable to those contained in the European Companies Statute with two exceptions. First, the management board is allowed to appoint its own chairman. Second, the supervisory board has been granted additional information rights where one-third of the supervisory board may obtain all relevant information and documents to undertake any necessary investigations.

In advancing its proposals, the EEC Commission considers the two-tier system as the best means for meeting both the needs of large modern enterprises and of society in general regarding such enterprises.[70] Moreover, the Commission has attempted to clarify the issue of appropriate forms and levels of worker participation within the enterprise by the following statement,

"The representation of employees on a company's supervisory body is only one form among others for participation in the economic and social affairs of the enterprise. It is additional to the negotiation of collective agreements, and to action, normally at establishment level, through employees' representative institutions, whether works councils or shop stewards. It complements these possibilities of intervention. Representation on a company's supervisory body adds a dimension otherwise lacking: an institution not only for the provision of information, and consultation on every important event, whether economic or social, but also the opportunity to influence effectively the decision making of the company on a continuing basis."[71]

To become effective, the Statute requires unanimous agreement in the Council while the Directive requires a sufficient majority as defined by the Community rules.[72] However, both proposals are still being debated by the member countries. There is no apprent agreement on the provisions for the supervisory board. Employer opinion has ranged from rejection of the principle to acceptance of one-third worker representation, whereas the trade unions tend to favour parity representation. A further problem has arisen with the accession of the United Kingdom into the EEC with no formal provisions for works councils. Consequently, it may be some time before either proposal is adopted by the Community.[73]

IV. Proposals For The United Kingdom

A. THE PRESENT SYSTEM

1. Collective Bargaining

The present industrial relations system in the United Kingdom tends to stand in contrast to most other West European systems. The main form of worker participation is through widespread collective bargaining generally focussing at the establishment level where negotiations occur between shop steward committees and management. However, collective bargaining in the United Kingdom is an essentially informal, voluntary process where companies are not required to recognize nor negotiate with trade unions and collective agreements are not legally binding.[74] As a result, although trade unions represent approximately forty-five per cent of the total labour force, their influence is inclined to vary greatly among enterprises and industries.[75] In addition, unions tend to be organized on an occupational basis, therefore certain groups of workers may not be represented even in unionized industries or enterprises. Where collective bargaining has become highly developed, the scope of bargainable issues is seen to be almost limitless.[76] Negotiations may include any question which the unions consider essential to their members' interests. Accordingly, most matters normally considered by the European works councils are covered by collective agreements in the United Kingdom. Still, certain major decisions affecting the enterprise, such as investments, closures, transfers and mergers are not usually the subject of negotiation.[77]

2.   Works Councils and Consultative Committees

Although there is no legislation requiring such representative institutions as works councils and consultative committees, various arrangements have been created under voluntary agreements between labour and management. These bodies generally perform only an advisory function and are precluded from dealing with any matters covered by a collective agreement. Moreover, they appear to be most important in industries or enterprises where unionization and shop steward representation is relatively weak or non-existent as shop stewards tend to reject the division of issues into those appropriate for consultation and those appropriate for negotiation.[78] However, successful arrangements have been established under trade union machinery with shop stewards forming the single channel for consultation and negotiation.[79]

3.   Company Structure and Worker Participation at Board Level

Present company law in the United Kingdom theoretically provides for a one-tier board structure composed of at least one director, who can be appointed or dismissed by the general shareholders' meeting. Under normal company articles of association, the board is empowered to perform managerial functions but may delegate its rights and responsibilities to certain persons or committees. Usually, these are board members who have been appointed executive directors by the board as a whole. The appointments and delegation of powers can be revoked or amended at any time subject to the particular articles of association. In addition, large enterprises frequently provide for the appointment of a specified number of "independent", non-executive board members.[80] Consequently, it has been observed that, in functional terms, many British companies actually operate under a two-tier system, where most managerial functions are performed by a small group of executive directors over whom the full board exercises a supervisory function.[81] In fact, present company law does not prohibit a two-tier structure which can be created through voluntary agreement under the company's articles of association.[82]

Company law stipulates the board of directors must act in the interests of the enterprise which are currently defined as those of the shareholders since employees are not legal company members. If directors attempt to safeguard other interests, such as employees, consumers or the general public, they may be held as acting illegally and can be challenged in court by a shareholder.[83] Thus, unless specifically provided for under the company's articles, management need not consider the implications of their decisions on employee welfare. Accordingly, worker representation in decision-making bodies is rare in the private sector, being confined to a few special organizations such as the John Lewis Partnership and the Scott Bader Commonwealth.[84]

In the public sector, nationalized industry boards normally include a member with a trade union background or a special understanding of employees' interests. However, it is also generally stipulated that no person shall be appointed if their interests will prejudicially affect the exercise of their functions as board members. Therefore, these members are not *direct* representatives of employees in the relevant enterprises, but are representatives of labour in general. In practice, the members are usually trade unionists no longer engaged in union activities or at least not in the industry concerned.[85] A noteworthy departure from this pattern is the recent agreement between the British Steel Corporation and the TUC Steel Committee which provides for the appointment of worker directors to the divisional boards of the corporation. Under this voluntary arrangement, the worker directors, who hold part-time non-executive positions, can be active trade union members in the steel industry. Individual unions within the industry submit candidate lists[86] to a joint selection panel comprised of the Steel Committee and BSC senior management. This panel in turn presents a short list to the Chairman of BSC who appoints the directors. Worker directors are entitled to participate in various joint consultative committees and, as board members, are responsible for approving or modifying policies submitted to the board. Still, worker influence over major issues tends to be limited as divisional boards are mainly advisory to the division managing director with executive decisions often taken at higher levels.[87]

B. MAJOR VIEWS AND PROPOSALS
FOR WORKER PARTICIPATION

Probably as a result of the United Kingdom becoming a member of the EEC as well as the growing recognition of a need for new methods to enhance labour-management relations, various organizations and political parties have put forward proposals to extend worker participation within the enterprise. Generally, most major groups seem to support the continued development and extension of collective bargaining as the primary form of worker participation in Britain.[88] However, there appears to be considerable disagreement concerning the appropriateness of other forms, including works councils and worker representation at board level, as well as the proper method of implementation. With respect to determining future legislation in this area, the views and proposals of the Trades Union Congress (TUC), the Labour Party, and the Confederation of British Industry (CBI) are of particular importance.[89]

1. The Trades Union Congress

At its 1974 Congress, the TUC formally adopted a set of proposals for extending worker influence over management decision making. The TUC has emphasized that any extension of industrial democracy must be based on widening trade union influence through the continued development of collective bargaining in all sectors of the economy and at various levels within the enterprise.[90] The main proposals may be summarized as follows,[91]

(i)   There should be a new Companies Act, to be introduced in stages, where initially all enterprises employing more than two thousand workers would have a two-tier board structure with the supervisory board responsible for determining company policy and appointing the management board.

(ii) Companies would be legally required to recognize and account for employees' as well as shareholders' interests.

(iii) One-half of the supervisory board members would be elected through trade union machinery, normally at company or combine level.

(iv) The above provisions concerning the supervisory board would only apply where there is trade union recognition, and representation of workers could only occur through bona fide trade unions choosing to exercise this right.

(v)   The Minister should be empowered to extend these provisions at a later stage to enterprises employing over 200 workers.

(vi) Nationalized inustries would also have fifty per cent trade union representation on the policy-making boards with the remaining fifty percent appointed by the Minister.

(vii) Legislation is required to ensure workers and their trade union representatives receive regular and detailed information on the activities of their enterprises.

(viii) A trade union would be entitled to apply for an arbitration award from the Conciliation and Arbitration Service (CAS) if an employer refused recognition.

The last two points are now covered under the Employment Protection Act where, for example, employers are obliged to inform and consult trade union representatives in redundancy situations and information agreements can be negotiated between unions and management. In addition, unions may bring recognition disputes to the CAS.[92]

Thus, the TUC has demanded that increased worker participation is to be obtained solely through trade union machinery. Accordingly, it has rejected the establishment of German or Dutch-type works councils, on the basis that they would merely duplicate existing plant-level collective bargaining machinery and may actually weaken union influence by creating a separate channel of communication between workers and management.[93] Moreover, it should be noted that the TUC believes worker representatives on the supervisory board should be directly responsible to the employees rather than the shareholders or company, although recently it has stated equal responsibility would be accepted given equal representation.[94] To avoid the risk of a deadlock between shareholder and worker representatives on the board, the TUC has suggested the following possible arrangements: a rotating chairman; joint co-option of a neutral member; or an independent chairman with a casting vote. However, it feels the preferable solution would be a bargained compromise acceptable to both groups.[95]

Finally, not all members of the TUC are in agreement with its proposals. Several of the larger unions, including the Electricians' Union, the Amalgamated Union of Engineering Workers, and the General and Municipal Workers' Union, would prefer participation through an extension of collective bargaining encompassing all company policy issues rather than through supervisory board representation.[96] Therefore, the TUC Congress also adopted a resolution rejecting the mandatory imposition of supervisory boards with worker directors but maintaining the need for permissive legislation granting unions the right to negotiate on major policy issues.

2. The Labour Party

The proposals of the Labour Party, as elaborated in its 1974 Green Paper on company law reform, are in general agreement with those of the TUC.[97] The paper emphasizes that, ". . . trade union participation at board level must be a supplement to, and not in any way detract from, the trade unions' position in collective bargaining", which, ". . . will remain the predominant method by which workers acquire a share of power in the private sector."[98] Therefore, it does not suggest the mandatory introduction of works councils as this would likely infringe upon the principle of single channel representation and may create a conflict with established patterns of collective bargaining.[99] The provisions for employee recognition as legal company members and a two-tier system with worker representation on the supervisory board are identical to those of the TUC. But, worker directors would be required to act in the interests of the enterprise as well as their constituency, with an equivalent duty placed on the shareholders' representatives. Finally, even though the Green Paper expresses a preference for the two-tier structure, it also observes that worker representatives on company boards could be viable under the existing one-tier system.

In the recent election campaign, the Labour party stated if re-elected, it planned to introduce worker participation legislation in a future parliamentary session. As the White Paper[100] on the subject states, it is no longer a question of 'if' but 'when and how' workers should be able to participate in decisions which can vitally affect their working lives and jobs. While the legislation will be influenced by the Bullock Committee inquiry on industrial democracy,[101] the intent is to proceed by voluntary agreements on a flexible company by company basis leaving the outcome to be shaped by experience.

If the proposals in the White Paper are accepted the government would prefer unions and employers to agree on their own participation schemes. However, where employees' ideas of 'adequate' participation differ from management's and voluntary agreement is impossible it is proposed that *legal fall backs* will be invoked in the form of two statutory participation rights,[102]

1. Employers in companies employing more than 500 workers in the United Kingdom should be under a legal obligation to discuss with employee representatives all major proposals affecting employees before decisions are made. Major policies such as investment plans, mergers, takeovers, expansion or contraction of establishments and major organizational changes are open for discussion with a Joint Representation Committee (JRC) representing all trade unions in the company.

2. After a JRC has gained three to four years of experience workers in companies employing over 2,000 employees will have the legal right to representation on boards of directors. If the parties cannot agree voluntarily on this issue, employees can then appoint one third of the directors to the supervisory board if a new two-tier corporate structure is adopted or to the existing unitary board of directors.

Given the division of opinion among British unions over the best way to proceed with participation, the proposed legislation offers sufficient flexibility to accommodate different views. Hard and fast rules about one or two-tier board systems are avoided although the two-tier Danish system (with workers on the top policy board) is favoured. Such a board would not be involved in the day to day running of the company - professionals will do this on the second board - but will be responsible for formulating company policy. The controversial question of parity representation on boards of directors is avoided unless companies voluntarily agree to it. And while it is assumed that the unions will dominate the participation process so that it does not conflict with normal collective bargaining, the rights of non-union members are considered. This is achieved by proposing that board-level representation can only be decided if a majority of all workers voting in a secret ballot agree to it and that JRC's be open to non-union members. In the event that unions object to the latter proposal, the company still remains free to consult the unorganized. If the interests of non-union workers are neglected at board level, they should have appeal rights (to a new industrial democracy commission?) and be free to nominate their own candidates.

3. The Confederation of British Industry

In contrast to TUC proposals, the Confederation of British Industry generally accepts *direct* forms of participation, such as job enrichment, improved communication and consultation within existing collective bargaining structures, but opposes indirect forms which imply the surrender of any management decision-making power.[103] Accordingly, it rejects the *mandatory* imposition of a two-tier board structure with worker directors, claiming that such a system is not relevant to the conditions and practices of British enterprises. It is also argued, worker directors would tend to become alienated from employees at establishment level as well as seriously impede the efficient functioning of the board.[104] Still, the CBI is willing to accept the principle of *voluntary* agreements for the establishment of supervisory boards or the appointment of worker directors under present company law.[105] Moreover, a 1973 CBI report[106] recommended that companies above a certain size should establish a consultative committee which is directly linked with the main company board. This link could be provided through an executive director nominated by the board to chair the committee and represent its views to the board. Information concerning company performance, investment plans, mergers and other major changes would be supplied to the committee for discussion. The purpose of this consultative arrangement would be to ensure that employees are confident their interests are considered by the board in its policy decisions. The report emphasizes effective forms of worker participation will not be obtained through legal coercion but through voluntary experimentation and evolution.[107]

In response to the 1974 TUC and Labour Party proposals, the CBI put forward the following recommendations:[108]

(i)   Companies employing more than 2,000 workers should negotiate participation agreements.

(ii)   If no agreement has been reached after four years, one could be legally enforced by a new tripartite agency, with the exception of requiring worker directors on a supervisory board.

(iii)   These voluntary or enforced agreements must conform with legislated guidelines.

(iv)   The agreements must be endorsed, through secret ballot, by all employees in the enterprise.

(v) Companies employing less than five hundred workers should establish company employee councils for the purpose of discussing efficiency, changes in internal structure, market conditions, new technology, investments, and sales policy.

Lastly, to meet the apparently inevitable introduction of worker directors in British industry, some members of the CBI have proposed the following system similar to the old German model:[109]

(i) Company boards should contain no more than one-third employee representatives.

(ii) Voting rights should not be confined exclusively to union members.

(iii) All board members are to be equally responsible for the conduct of the company and must maintain confidentiality requirements.

(iv) Complementary arrangements for worker participation must be created below board level.

Consequently, it can be seen that management and labour maintain widely divergent views concerning the appropriate forms of worker participation to be introduced in the United Kingdom. Whereas the CBI tends to support voluntary consultative arrangements at establishment level, the TUC advocates *equal* participation in decision making at board level. The above discussion of the various proposals would seem to indicate that a relatively unique system of worker participation will evolve in an attempt to incorporate it into the highly developed collective bargaining context. The final result will primarily depend on the relative power or influence of the concerned parties. Yet, from the successful West German experience, it would appear that an effective system of worker participation necessitates the establishment of complementary forms at all levels within the enterprise, taking into account the particular characteristics of the industrial relations system. Commenting on the many lost opportunities in British industrial relations since World War II *The Economist* makes the point that industrialists are probably wrong in their exaggerated fears of worker directors. To think of the worker director - or of joint discussion of major items of company strategy - as posing nothing but problems, and not also opportunities, contradicts much foreign experience. It plays into the hands of those who see industry as nothing but a class battlefield, transforming the conflicts of interest that do genuinely exist into a total conflict of interest on all points. Does anyone think British industries and boardrooms perform so brilliantly that such a change through compromise must be for the worse?[110] Is there a lesson in the above assertions for Canada?

Notes

[1] Loew, W., "National Report, Germany", *Prospects for Labour/Management Co-operation in the Enterprise,* Paris, OECD, 1974, p.97.

[2] CIR, *Worker Participation and Collective Bargaining in Europe,* Her Majesty's Stationery Office, 1974, p.12.

[3] Shutt, H., ed., *Worker Participation in West Germany, Sweden, Yugoslavia, and the United Kingdom,* London, The Economist Intelligence Unit, 1975, p.9; CIR, *op. cit.,* p.12.

[4] European Communities Commission, *Employee Participation and Company Structure in the European Community.* Supplement 8/75, p.58.

[5] Connaghan, C.J., *Partnership or Marriage of Convenience?,* Ottawa, Labour Canada, 1976, p.7.

[6] CIR, *op. cit.,* p.13.

[7] Connaghan, *op. cit.,* p.8.

[8] Connaghan, *op. cit.,* p.10; CIR, *op. cit.,* p.13.

[9] Connaghan, *op. cit.,* pp.21-22.

[10] CIR, *op. cit.,* p.12.

[11] Shutt, *op. cit.,* p. 9; CIR, *op. cit.,* p.12; Connaghan, *op. cit.,* pp.13-14.

[12] Both the federal and provincial governments have jurisdiction over labour legislation but the Basic Law of Germany and actual practice stipulate that federal jurisdiction takes precedence. See Connaghan, *op. cit.* p.25.

[13] The Labour Courts operate at three levels: the Local Court where all actions are initiated; the Provincial Court which is the first level of appeal; and the Federal Court being the supreme level of appeal.

[14] CIR, *op. cit.,* pp.13-14.

[15] Connaghan, *op. cit.*, pp.22-23.

[16] Connaghan, *op. cit.*, pp.22-23.

[17] Connaghan, *op. cit.*, pp.22-23.

[18] Approximately 8,000 collective agreements are concluded each year. European Communities Commission, *op. cit.*, p.58.

[19] European Communities Commission, *op. cit.*, p.58; CIR, *op. cit.*, p.15; Connaghan, *op. cit.*, pp.14,16.

[20] European Communities Commission, *op. cit.*, p. 58.

[21] This Act is an amendment to the original Works Constitution Act of 1952 which created the works council and employee representation on supervisory boards of companies outside the coal, iron and steel industries.

[22] International Labour Organization, *Participation of Workers in Decisions Within Undertakings*, Labour-Management Series: NO. 33, Geneva, International Labour Office, 1969, p.56; European Communities Commission, *op. cit.*, p.59.

[23] Loew, *op. cit.*, p.98.

[24] European Communities Commission, *op. cit.*, p.59.

[25] Connaghan, *op. cit.*, p.68; ILO, 1969, *op. cit.*, p.56; CIR, *op. cit.*, p.23.

[26] European Communities Commission, *op. cit.*, p.59.

[27] European Communities Commission, *op. cit.*, p.59; Loew, *op. cit.*, pp.99-100.

[28] European Communities Commission, *op. cit.*, p.59.

[29] Loew, *op. cit.*, p.100; Connaghan, *op. cit.*, pp.68-69

[30] Loew, *op. cit.*, pp.100-103; European Communities Commission, *op. cit.*, pp.59-60, Connaghan, *op. cit.*, pp. 69-70.

[31] Loew, *op. cit.*, p.106; European Communities Commission, *op. cit.*, p.60.

[32] Enterprises operating under this structure would include public companies, private limited liability companies, mutual insurance companies and co-operative societies employing more than five hundred workers. Connaghan, *op. cit.*, p.71.

[33] European Communities Commission, *op. cit.*, pp.64-65.

[34] Connaghan, *op. cit.*, p.72; European Communities Commission, *op. cit.*, pp.65-66; Loew, *op. cit.*, p.1-3.

[35] European Communities Commission, *op. cit.*, p.62.

[36] This Act has its origin in the post-war period when occupational forces limited strictly the powers of the strategic mining and steel corporations. In 1947, British authorities, with the agreement of the German trade unions, introduced a system of co-determination in administering these companies. The former owners, anxious to regain at least partial control, did not oppose the scheme. When the Republic of Germany formulated its own legislation for the industry, the trade unions insisted on preserving their existing status. European Communities Commissions, *op. cit.*, pp.61-62.

[37] Loew, *op. cit.*, p.103; European Communities Commission, *op. cit.*, pp.61-62.

[38] Loew, *op. cit.*, p.103.

[39] Shutt, *op. cit.*, pp.12-13; European Communities Commission, *op. cit.*, pp.62-63; Connaghan, *op. cit.*, pp.72-73.

[40] Shutt, *op. cit.*, p.13; European Communities Commission, *op. cit.*, p.63.

[41] Shutt, *op. cit.*, p.9; Connaghan, *op. cit.*, p.73; ILO 1969, *op. cit.*, p.47.

[42] Bavinck, J.G. and deLeeuw, M., "National Report, The Netherland", *Prospects for Labour/Management Co-operation in the Enterprise*, Paris, OECD. 1974, pp.135-136.

[43] CIR, *op. cit.*, p.59.

[44] The NVV is comprised of 19 unions; the NKV, 24; and the CNV, 25. The NVV and NKV tend to act as one organization and are presently discussing a merger. CIR, *op. cit.*, pp.59-60.

[45] CIR, *op. cit.*, pp.59,62; Dufty, N.F., *Changes in Labour-Management Relations in the Enterprise*, Paris, OECD, 1975, p.15.

[46] Bavinck and deLeeuw, *op. cit.*, p.147; Dufty, *op. cit.*, p.14.

[47] CIR, *op. cit.*, p.58.

[48] CIR, *op. cit.*, pp.61-62; Bavinck and deLeeuw, *op. cit.*, p.137.

[49] European Communities Commission, *op. cit.*, p.89; Bavinck and deLeeuw, *op. cit.*, p.146.

[50] CIR, *op. cit.*, p.62; European Communities Commission, *op. cit*, p.88; Dufty, *op. cit.*, p.14.

[51] Bavinck and deLeeuw, *op. cit.*, p.139.

[52] Bavinck and deLeeuw, *op. cit.*, pp.148-149.

[53] European Communities Commission, *op. cit.*, p.89; Bavinck and deLeeuw, *op. cit.*, p.142.

[54] European Communities Commission, *op. cit.*, p.89; Bavinck and deLeeuw, *op. cit.*, pp.142-144.

[55] European Communities Commission, *op. cit.*, p.89; Bavinck and deLeeuw, *op. cit.*, pp.140-142; CIR, *op. cit.*, p.67.

[56] Bavinck and deLeeuw, *op. cit.*, pp.149,152.

[57] Bavinck and deLeeuw, *op. cit.*, p.145; European Communities Commission, *op. cit.*, p.90.

[58] Bavinck and deLeeuw, *op. cit.*, p.149; European Communities Commission, *op. cit.*, p.90.

[59] This Act came into force in 1973.

[60] Bavinck and deLeeuw, *op. cit.*, p.145; European Communities Commission, *op. cit.*, pp.91-92.

[61] European Communities Commission, *op. cit.*, p.92.

[62] European Communities Commission, *op. cit.*, pp.90-91; Bavinck and deLeeuw, *op. cit.*, pp.144-145.

[63] Bavinck and deLeeuw, *op. cit.*, p.145.

[64] European Communities Commission, *op. cit.*, p.91.

[65] For the various union proposals, see CIR, *op. cit.*, p.65 and Bavinck and deLeeuw, *op. cit.*, pp.149-150.

[66] European Communities Commission, *op. cit.*, p.40.

[67] Shutt, *op. cit.*, p.48; CIR, p.7.

[68] Unless otherwise noted, the following description of the Statute and Directive is based on that provided by the CIR report, pp.8-10 and the European Communities Commission, *op. cit.*, p.107.

[69] The supervisory board will not include worker representatives if two-thirds of the employees in the enterprise do not desire such participation.

[70] European Communities Commission, *op. cit.*, p.40. For a discussion of the arguments in support of the two-tier system, see European Communities Commission, *op. cit.*, pp.16-20.

[71] European Communities Commission, *op. cit.*, p.41.

[72] CIR, *op. cit.*, p.7.

[73] CIR, *op. cit.*, p.10.

[74] Cobb, M. and Graham, K., "National Report, United Kingdom", *Prospects for Labour/Management Co-operation in the Enterprise*, Paris, OECD, 1974, p.183; Lloyd, G. and Cannell, *Workers' Participation in Decisions Within Undertakings in the United Kingdom*, Geneva, International Labour Office, 1974, p.5; European Communities Commission, *op. cit.*, p.93.

[75] Shutt, *op. cit.*, p.33.

[76] Cobb and Graham, *op. cit.*, p.184; European Communities Commission, *op. cit.*, p.93.

[77] European Communities Commission, *op. cit.*, p.94.

[78] Cobb and Graham, *op. cit.*, p.189.

[79] European Communities Commission, *op. cit.*, p.96.

[80] *The Community and the Company: Reform of Company Law*, Report of a Working Group of the Labour Party Industrial Policy Sub-Committee, London, The Labour Party, 1974, p.13; European Communities Commission, *op. cit.*, pp.100-101.

[81] *The Community and the Company*, *op. cit.*, p.13; European Communities Commission, *op. cit.*, p.101. A 1971 survey of two hundred and forty-three large British companies revealed that a typical board contained between six and fifteen members where eighty per cent of the boards provided for the appointment of non-executive directors who comprised between one-quarter to one-third of total membership. European Communities Commission, *op. cit.*, p.101.

[82] European Communities Commission, *op. cit.,* pp.100,101.

[83] *The Community and the Company, op. cit.,* p.10; European Communities Commission, *op. cit.,* p.100.

[84] European Communities Commpssion, *op. cit.,* p.97.

[85] European Communities Commission, *op. cit.,* p.97; Lloyd and Cannell, *op. cit.,* p.3.

[86] Each union is permitted to choose its own method of selecting its candidates.

[87] Garnett, J., *Democracy in Industry,* London, The Industrial Society, 1976, pp.27-29; European Communities Commission, *op. cit.,* p.97; Lloyd and Cannell, *op. cit.,* p.4.

[88] European Communities Commission, *op. cit.,* pp.94-95.

[89] The TUC and CBI are respectively the major national labour and management organizations in Britain.

[90] Lloyd and Cannell, *op. cit.,* p.9; European Communities Commission, *op. cit.,* pp.94-95.

[91] Lloyd and Cannell, *op. cit.,* pp.5-10; Shutt, *op. cit.,* p.35.

[92] "The workers at the boardroom door", *The Economist,* September 4, 1976, p.91; European Communities Commission, *op. cit.,* pp.94,96.

[93] Lloyd and Cannell, *op. cit.* p.7; *The Economist, op. cit.,* p.82; Shutt, *op. cit.,* p.36; *The Community and the Company, op. cit.,* pp.11-12.

[94] Lloyd and Cannell, *op. cit.,* p.7; *The Economist, op. cit.,* p.79.

[95] *The Economist, op. cit.,* p.79.

[96] Shutt, *op. cit.,* p.36; *The Economist, op. cit.,* p.79; European Communities Commission, *op. cit.,.,* p.98.

[97] See *The Community and the Company, op. cit.,* pp.10-17.

[98] *The Community and the Company, op. cit.,* p.12.

[99] *The Community and the Company, op. cit.,* p.11.

[100] Cmnd. 7231. *Industrial Democracy,* London, H.M.S.O., May, 1978.

[101] Cmnd. 6706. *Report of the Committee of Inquiry on Industrial Democracy,* London, H.M.S.O., January, 1977.

[102] Cmnd. 7231, *op. cit.,* p.2,3.

[103] Garnett, J., *Practical Policies for Participation,* London, The Industrial Society, 1974, p.22; Shutt, *op. cit.,* pp.38-39; *The Economist, op. cit.,* pp.79,80.

[104] Garnett, J., 1974, *op. cit.,* p.21; *The Economist, op. cit.,* p.80.

[105] Garnett. J., 1974, *op. cit.,* p.22; European Communities Commission, *op. cit.,* p.98.

[106] *The Responsibilities of the British Company,* London, CBI, 1973. See also, Garnett, J., 1974, *op. cit.* p.22.

[107] Garnett, J., 1974, *op. cit.,* p.22.

[108] *The Economist, op. cit.,* p.80.

[109] *The Economist, op. cit.,* p.80.

[110] *The Economist,* May 27, 1978, p.78.

III

Advantages and Disadvantages of Worker Participation: Potential Obstacles to Its Introduction in Canada

The preceding description of several West European models and proposals would indicate no uniform system of worker participation could be applied with equal success across nations due to differing political, economic and social contexts. Suitable forms must be designed to accommodate the particular needs of the country and perhaps the special requirements of individual industries or enterprises within that country.[1] At the same time it should be recognized that the concept of worker participation as a feasible means of realizing rising worker aspirations and enhancing labour-management relations cannot be expected to resolve every problem which may arise in an industrial relations system. In fact, there presently exists considerable controversy over the possible advantages and disadvantages of worker participation itself. Consequently, the West European experience will be reviewed in an attempt to assess these perceived advantages or disadvantages and to indicate potential obstacles to introducing a similar system within the Canadian context.

I. The West European Experience

There appears to be a great diversity of attitudes toward the relative benefits and costs of worker participation in Western Europe. This is particularly evident with respect to certain forms and the actual degree of worker involvement in decision-making. Yet the success of any system of participation will be highly dependent on its acceptance by both labour and management. Therefore, a general discussion of the prevalent European labour-management attitudes will be presented followed by some evidence concerning the economic and social impact of participation.

A.   ATTITUDES TOWARD PARTICIPATION

1. Labour

Although it has been observed that workers' attitudes toward participation will vary according to their values, ideologies, age, sex, skill, education and experience,[2] several surveys from different countries indicate a majority of employees favour the general concept of participation in managerial decision-making.[3] Where provision has been made for works councils and representation on company boards, most employees appear to support these institutions. For example, a study conducted on three hundred and thirty German enterprises operating under the 1952 Works Constitution Act found sixty-seven percent of interviewed employees expressed a positive view that the works councils were effective. Ninety-two percent stated they could not do without the institution. Employees were also found to have a greater interest in matters which directly affected them as opposed to those council activities which were associated with administrative regulations.[4] At the same time, a relatively small proportion of employees appear to be interested in personally participating in these institutions. Rather, they tend to be much more interested in personally influencing decisions which are directly related to their own work situation. Additionally, the findings that workers usually have limited knowledge regarding the functioning of their representative institutions, have often been taken to imply that employees are primarily concerned with direct forms of participation. But it has been countered that workers are not so much interested in the *processes* of indirect participation as in the *outcomes* of these processes; specifically, the protection of their jobs and income. The absence of detailed knowledge does not mean lack of support for such institutions as trade unions, works councils and board representation.[5] Employees' desire to exercise greater control has been clearly manifested in the past several years through spontaneous demonstrations in the form of "sit-ins", "work-ins" and "wildcat" strikes.[6] Therefore, it has been argued that management policies based solely on direct participation could lead to serious repercussions as indirect forms are also necessary in order to fully serve all of the workers' perceived needs.[7]

The attitudes of the European trade unions toward participation appear to vary according to their stated ideologies. Radical socialist and communist unions in Belgium, France, and Italy have commonly opposed worker participation on the principle that it would substitute class collaboration for the class struggle and thus it is incompatible with their philosophy of rejecting capitalism. These unions either advocate the nationalization of industries or a system of full workers' control over enterprises similar to that operating in Yugoslavia.[8] In addition, more moderate unions supporting an adversary or private enterprise philosophy have expressed the fear that developments toward greater worker participation might compromise the union's independence as a bargaining organization. While they wish to be fully informed, consulted and empowered to bargain over a maximum range of issues on behalf of their members, the unions do not want to share responsibility for decisions taken by management. Such a sharing of responsibility could involve a serious conflict of interest for the worker representative who would be expected to advance the interests of the enterprise as well as the interests of workers. Thus, an official of the Electrical Trades Union in Great Britain has stated, "It is not the duty of the trade unionists to participate. Their duty is to protect and advance the interests of their members."[9]Moreover, certain union organizations, notably the Trades Union Congress, have rejected any form of participation which is independent of trade union machinery on the grounds that it would undermine the union's influence and effectiveness as a representative organization.[10]

Worker participation appears to be most strongly supported by trade unions which are largely integrated in the existing society, associated with its aims, and closely identified with social democratic political parties, as in the case of the West German, Dutch, Norwegian, Swedish, and Danish unions.[11] Board representation and works councils are often seen as an essential means of influencing management decisions at the enterprise level and a valuable source of information for collective bargaining purposes. [12] Thus, these institutions are usually viewed as complementary to, rather than in conflict with, the collective bargaining function which frequently focusses at the industry or national level. However, there is a common dissatisfaction with the present consultative nature of most works councils where the unions are now demanding greater decision-making powers. Furthermore these unions are pressing increasingly for a system of parity representation on company boards similar to the German mining and steel industry model. In fact, this would seem to be a growing trend within the West European labour movement, excluding the radical and communist unions.[13]

2. Management

While European employers normally accept the general principle of involving workers in decision-making processes, they usually resist any surrender of traditional managerial prerogatives. Accordingly, management is inclined to support participative arrangements which are primarily consultative in nature or concerned with decisions directly related to the execution of workers' tasks.[14] In this respect, employers seem to favour works councils as an effective means of facilitating communication and cooperation between labour and management but have tended to oppose the extension of council co-decision rights.[15] Management has also frequently initiated the development of autonomous work groups for the purpose of improving workers' job satisfaction and performance. In emphasizing the importance of direct forms of participation, managers often present the argument that employees are interested mainly in obtaining more responsibility and control over the performance of their tasks.[16]

Consistent with the desire to maintain their decision-making freedom, management is less favourably disposed towards worker participation at board level. In addition to West Germany and the Netherlands, Austria, Denmark, Sweden, Norway, France and Luxembourg have introduced various arrangements for minority worker representation on company boards. Employers in these countries seem to evaluate their experience with minority representation fairly positively where it is seen as a means of informing employees on the enterprise's economic situation which in turn has encouraged cooperation with management proposals.[17] But there is almost unanimous opposition to any form of parity representation with shareholders losing their majority position. Numerous arguments have been presented in support of this position.[18] The most prevalent is the claim that co-determination will seriously reduce enterprise efficiency by restricting excessively the managerial freedom necessary for rapid decisions in adjusting to changing economic conditions. Also, the firm's ability to attract new investment may be inhibited if employee representatives pursue a policy of preserving existing structures and jobs rather than a policy of maximizing profits through innovation and efficiency improvements. Accordingly, many employers reject the analogy between political and industrial democracy and assert that, ". . . companies must be managed according to the laws of economic efficiency, not the principle of political compromise."[19] It is argued, in a capitalist system management must be responsible first to the shareholders or owners of the enterprise, yet this may be jeopardized if important decisions are subject to agreement among groups with divergent interests and possible political concepts. Moreover, it is feared co-determination may provide trade unions with excessive power, threatening the autonomy of the collective bargaining partners and raising the question of the union's role in a free market economy. It has been alleged that such worker dominance would entail a fundamental change in property structures which would endanger the future development of the free enterprise system.[20]

From the above discussion it would seem there is still a substantial divergence in attitudes between management and labour concerning worker participation. Whereas unions who support the concept emphasize the need for increased co-decision rights through indirect forms of participation, management tends to endorse consultative and direct forms. Still, it has already been noted that attitudes are not static but subject to change as conditions change. Attitudes may be transformed through experience with particular forms of participation as well as evolutions in the political, economic and social environment. Thus, in terms of the European context it has been observed,[21]

> . . . the moderate position on worker participation usually envisions at least one-third worker representation on boards of directors, frequently combined with concessions increasing works council powers and worker participation in capital. Only a few years ago this would have been regarded as the most that might be expected in European labour relations; today it seems the least.

B. ECONOMIC AND SOCIAL IMPACT OF PARTICIPATION

Unfortunately there have been very few comprehensive analyses on the economic and social consequences of worker participation in Western Europe. This is probably at least partly due to the inherent difficulties involved in attempting a comparative analysis of the different systems.[22] For example, there is an initial problem in developing some objective measure for the impact of worker participation, particularly with respect to the social effects. It will also be very difficult to estimate the economic impact of participation due to the problem of isolating its effects from the complexity of factors which influence a firm's performance. Moreover, the impact of a given form of participation may depend critically on the specific political, social, and economic environment.[23] Finally, with the exception of West Germany, available evidence is extremely limited as most European countries have only recently established formal institutions for employee involvement in decision-making processes. As a result, it is often necessary to rely on the opinion of those involved in worker participation for assessing its validity as a means of improving labour-management relations and promoting economic efficiency.

1.   Economic Impact

There appears to be no clear agreement whether the total impact of worker participation on enterprise efficiency has been positive, negative or neutral since it is exceedingly difficult to isolate all of the direct and indirect effects. With respect to participation on company boards, evidence from West Germany would seem to indicate that worker directors have had little direct effect on the efficiency of enterprises or their competitive position.[24] Although there have been accusations of coalition formation which have led to reductions in efficiency within the mining and steel industry, little or no concrete evidence has been presented to support these contentions. A German government inquiry conducted by the Biedenkopf Commission found that co-determination had seldom prevented the implementation of management proposals and unanimous votes within the supervisory board were the rule rather than the exception.[25] Similarly, worker directors in firms coming under the works constitution act do not appear to have impeded such decisions as mergers or investments which directly and adversely affected employees. This may be a consequence of the requirement that all board members be responsible to the interests of the enterprise rather than to group interests and trade union acceptance of the profit motive as a guideline for decision-making.[26] Thus, a recent study has observed that, even though an original union justification for worker participation on company boards was the prevention of concentrated industries, the overriding goals of providing higher living standards and long-term employment security have allowed unions to accept the argument that large industrial units are necessary for effective competition in international markets. These union goals are seen to have greatly facilitated co-operation with management proposals.[27] However, it should also be noted, prior to 1975 employee directors outside the mining and steel industry had limited powers as a result of their minority position on the board. Consequently, any attempts to introduce policies having a detrimental effect on enterprise efficiency could be blocked by the shareholder-elected majority. The power of worker representatives was further restricted in many cases when shareholder directors held their own preliminary meeting to discuss major issues before presenting these to the board.[28]

At the same time, it is often claimed worker participation on supervisory boards has led to considerable improvements in alleviating the adverse impact of enterprise decisions on employees through the implementation of social plans.[29] These plans may include such measures as phased redundancy arrangements, compensation terms, redeployment devices and the creation of new jobs. While the social plan constitutes a direct cost to the enterprise, it may be argued that the benefits derived by affected employees and the probable decrease in indirect costs - through reducing potential industrial conflict - may offset these direct costs. The successful rationalization of the German mining and steel industry is usually cited in support of this argument. The co-determination system was considered to be an essential factor in minimizing conflict during a twenty year period of substantial rationalization, closures and mergers which resulted in the elimination of four hundred thousand jobs. Union leaders claim these changes were accomplished with little industrial unrest because worker directors insisted on generous redundancy pay and the provision of new jobs.[30] From the relatively successful experience of the mining and steel industry, N. F. Dufty concludes that the new system of near parity representation provided by the 1975 Works Constitution Act is unlikely to damage enterprise efficiency and may even make a positive contribution. However, he additionally argues that the TUC proposals for parity representation with worker directors directly responsible to union members' interests may reduce efficiency as they could create opportunities for "doctrinaire harassing tactics" in particular circumstances.[31]

Again, owing to the lack of adequate studies, there is little clear evidence to assess the economic impact of works councils. It may be reasoned that works councils which are primarily limited to a consultative role (as is the case in most West European countries), will not adversely affect enterprise efficiency and may actually have a positive influence through the exchange of information and ideas.

However, Dufty argues that the present trend towards extending council powers over issues affecting current or future employment prospects is likely to have a negative impact on efficiency, the rate of technological change, and resource allocation. In an attempt to protect existing jobs and employment structures, works councils may force management to continue operating inefficient plants and equipment and inhibit the transfer of labour from areas where its net marginal value productivity is low to those areas where it is comparatively high.[32] Yet, C. J. Connaghan's analysis of the West German system of participation which presently includes the most powerful works councils in Western Europe would seem to counter this argument. Connaghan sees the post-war reconstruction of Germany and its recognition today as one of Europe's most stable economies as largely the result of its labour-management system.[33] During the 1974-75 world recession, Germany displayed one of the strongest economic performances in the EEC where its GNP rose by 0.4 percent compared to a general decline in most other Western countries; it experienced the second lowest inflation rate in the Community (which was approximately one half the Canadian and one-fifth the British rate) while enjoying one of the highest living standards in the world; it maintained a trade balance surplus when its trading partners, including the United States, suffered deficits; and the value of the deutsche mark in terms of U.S. dollars appreciated by more than fifty-two percent.[34] From this evidence, it might be inferred that if the German works councils did in fact inhibit efficiency improvements, the rate of technological change and potential productivity levels, the effect was probably only marginal. Furthermore, the Commission on Industrial Relations found German employers generally consider the councils as essential and conducive to effective management where,

> . . . many managers take the view that the works councils make them more efficient than they would otherwise be on the grounds that good human relations makes for an efficient firm.[35]

It may also be argued that where board representation and works council provisions reduce the conflictual element of labour-management relations (by enabling unions to reach their objectives through means other than confrontation), enterprise efficiency may improve as a result of fewer work stoppages and restrictive labour practices.[36] The following table[37] would seem to suggest a negative correlation between the number of days lost through industrial disputes and the extent of participative arrangements.

TABLE I INDUSTRIAL DISPUTES

Average No. of days lost per 1,000 persons employed

Country	1969	1970	1961-5	1966-70	1961-70
France	200	190	340	265(a)	306(b)
Germany	20	10	34	12	23
Italy	4,100	1,500	1,200	966	1,093
Belgium	100	870	130	322	226
Netherlands	10	140	16	34	25
Norway		70	212	18	115
Denmark	70	160	768	60	414
Ireland	2,150	480	1,002	1,096	1,049
U.K.	520	740	238	404	321

(a) and (b). These figures omit 1968 which was a year of large scale, semi-political strikes in France. Adapted from *Department of Employment Gazette,* December 1971, p.1167.

It can be determined from the table that the United Kingdom, Ireland and Italy which tend to emphasize collective bargaining as the principal means of influencing management decisions, have a significantly higher number of days lost due to industrial conflict than Germany and the Netherlands with extensive formal representative institutions.

Moreover, for the decade ending 1977 Germany has had one of the lowest strike records in the western countries. For example, per one thousand employees for every fifty-three days lost annually by German workers, French workers lost two hundred and eighty days, British workers eight hundred and fifty days, Italian workers one thousand nine hundred and fourteen days, United States workers one thousand three hundred and forty days and Canadian workers one thousand eight hundred and ninety days.[38] Consequently, there does seem to be some evidence supporting the proposition that board representation and works councils may have a positive indirect impact on enterprise efficiency through a reduction in labour-management conflict.

Finally, it has been argued that worker participation may indirectly increase efficiency by improving worker satisfaction resulting in higher worker productivity, lower labour turnover and absenteeism.[39] Present evidence suggests board representation and works councils have not affected appreciably worker satisfaction, perhaps because these institutions are too far removed from the employees' immediate concerns at the level of the workplace.[40] Conversely, numerous studies have concluded that direct forms of participation (job enrichment, enlargement and reorganization schemes) have clearly produced a positive effect on enterprise efficiency as a result of significantly reduced labour turnover and absenteeism levels.[41] Moreover, these forms, especially autonomous groups, have been found to raise worker productivity, although this may be a consequence of changes in work organization rather than greater job satisfaction.

From the limited evidence, it would appear that worker participation may have a positive impact on the economic situation of the firm, or at worst, no deleterious effect. The European Communities Commission has contended,[42]

> . . . if one compares the positions in different Member States, it certainly cannot be said that there is an apparent correlation between regimes of employee participation and situations of low efficiency, low profits and inadequate investment. If anything these problems seem more closely associated with the existence of industrial relations systems in which there is little or no formal employee participation, and a relatively high incidence of industrial confrontation. Though a causal connection cannot be scientifically established, this observation would suggest that social conflict, resulting in part from the exclusion of employees from decision-making, is a greater threat to efficiency and investment than a degree of employee participation.

The Commission further argues that the notion of efficiency should be broadened to include not only the traditional concept of relative financial returns on the capital invested in particular enterprises but also other elements which account for the general welfare of society. For example, the cost of industrial confrontation should be imputed from the social-economic system as a whole as well as for the particular enterprise in which it occurs. Regarded in these terms, there is little basis for the argument that increased worker participation will necessarily lead to decreased efficiency. Still, the Commission notes an efficiency problem may arise if participation is organized in a way that permits employee representatives to unilaterally block the implementation of major economic decisions.[43]

2. Social Impact

While it is difficult to detect the immediate economic impact of participation, there appears to be widespread agreement that it has an unquestionably positive influence on social policy issues and human relationships within the enterprise. Even though the average employee may have little detailed knowledge about the actual operation of the participative machinery, there is a common consensus in West Germany that worker participation has made a major contribution to the humanization of relations between the various participants in production.[44] In pressing for a general extension of co-determination, the DGB has argued the system operating in the mining and steel industry has greatly improved communication in the enterprise, broken down authoritarian attitudes and reduced the anonymity of management. Arrangements for employee representatives on the supervisory board also ensures that management is made aware of workers' interests and likely reactions so that decisions are based on social as well as economic considerations and provision is made for the social costs involved.[45] Moreover, the West European unions usually view the works council system as an important check on management actions while management often considers it as an effective means of carrying out policies with a minimum of conflict.[46] Although it has been contended management may attempt to manipulate the works council for its own purposes, their ability to do so is often limited by the high degree of union representation in the councils.[47] For example, in Germany, Belgium and the Netherlands, approximately eighty percent of the council members belong to trade unions. Still, an important criticism of the works councils is their tendency to become bureaucratic, which can create difficulties in maintaining communications between the council and employees. To the extent this occurs, employee alienation and dissatisfaction may actually increase as council activities fail to correspond with workers' concerns and expectations.[48]

Studies on direct forms of participation have revealed a vital contribution towards mutual understanding between management and employees. Moreover, the proven ability of these schemes to reduce worker alienation and improve job satisfaction has been regarded as an important social result in addition to the positive effect on efficiency.[49] Accordingly, management often feels the introduction of greater worker involvement at the level of the task is an essential precondition for the successful operation of participative arrangements at higher levels.[50]

Thus, it would seem that worker participation has provided a valuable contribution to enhanced human relations within the enterprise. From their study, Walker and de Bellecombe have concluded,[51]

> Without having been divided at its source, authority has lost some of its absolutism . . . in the new context in which it is exercised, the people subject to it show themselves more willing than in the past to recognise it as a necessity of a technical sort, justified by the differences in reponsibility, instead of submitting to it as an arbitrary constraint bound up merely with subordination to a hierarchy.

This evolution is seen to have a very favourable impact on the atmosphere within the enterprise, contributing to stability in labour-management relations. Furthermore, Walker has observed that the introduction of worker participation does not necessarily imply a simple transfer of power from management to employees. The actual effect may be to increase the total amount of control as a participative structure brings under direct command certain events which were previously uncontrolled or subject to the unilateral discretion of managers or workers.[52] Hence, West European evidence seems to demonstrate that worker participation is a viable means of accommodating rising employee aspirations for more meaningful work and greater involvement in the decision-making process while at the same time allowing for efficient management of the enterprise.

II. Obstacles to Introducing Worker Participation in Canada

Experiences with present participative arrangements suggest a program incorporating supervisory board representation and effective works councils (as well as encouraging the development of collective bargaining) can make a unique contribution to improved industrial relations. But such a program must be designed to meet the particular requirements of a country's political-social-economic context. The successful development of participative institutions necessitates considerations of such factors as the industrial relations system, the structure and role of workers' and employers' organizations, the structural or legal relationship between the factors of production, and the basic socio-cultural characteristics of the population. In addition, it is highly unlikely that a comprehensive system of worker participation could be introduced without encountering certain initial problems and obstacles. The more participation requires a marked departure from traditional values and authority structures, the more problems may be expected during its introduction as labour and management are required to adapt to the new situations.[53] In terms of the Canadian context, several important legal and institutional obstacles to introducing participation should be discussed. Unfortunately, there exists very little analysis concerned with the applicability of worker participation to the Canadian situation.[54] Therefore, some of the potential obstacles will be inferred from the American and British contexts which have highly similar industrial relations systems.

A. LEGAL OBSTACLES

1. Company Structure

The European Communities Commission has found employee representation on company boards is most developed in those countries where enterprises have a two-tier board structure. Part of the explanation may be the ability of a dualist structure to formally separate functions, enabling the representation of a plurality of interests to be combined with a homogeneous management in a way unitary systems find difficult to duplicate.[55] Present Canadian company law approximates that of the United Kingdom which at least theoretically provides for a one-tier board structure. As a result, Canada may be expected to encounter similar legal issues regarding the introduction of worker participation as those previously discussed for the United Kingdom. Therefore, it may be necessary to reform company law in a way that strengthens both the employees' and public's interest; redefines the duties and responsibilities of directors, with particular reference to employee representatives; and ensures the directors possess real rather than theoretical power to supervise management activities.[56] With respect to employee representation at board level, three controversial issues must be resolved: who will represent the workers; the method of election, and the relative number of worker representatives. Analogous to the British debate, it can be expected that Canadian unions will demand direct involvement in the selection process and employers will reject any scheme providing for parity representation.

As in the British case, there will likely be considerable opposition in Canada to the mandatory imposition of a two-tier board structure. The European Communities Commission has acknowledged that countries with strong industrial and commercial traditions having one board systems may experience substantial difficulties if they attempt an immediate introduction of the two-tier model. Yet, it is felt these difficulties may owe more to fears deriving from present lack of knowledge than to any inherent disadvantage of the system. To alleviate this problem, the Commission proposes the use of a transitional solution where a clear separation of function and responsibility would be initially established between the "managers" and "supervisors" on a unitary board.[57] This approach should be considered seriously if the Canadian government desires to implement two-tier boards with a minimum of potential conflict.

2. Government Legislation

It has become apparent there is an urgent need for changes in current Canadian labour policy and legislation. The excessive number of man-days lost due to industrial disputes has revealed that the adversary approach, as maintained by present legislation, is neither conducive to stable labour-management relations nor steady economic growth. Still, the Federal and Provincial governments do not seem to have made any serious attempts at major innovations in the Canadian industrial relations system for the last decade. An important explanation of this situation is probably the political problems involved in introducing reforms which substantially deviate from the traditional system. Hence, it will presumably take a long period of time to implement such a fundamental change as worker participation which emphasizes cooperation and consultation as opposed to confrontation. Yet, government initiative will likely be required if a system of worker participation is to be developed in Canada. For example, experiments in appropriate participative arrangements may be initially conducted in crown corporations setting a pattern for private industry to follow.

A further problem arises from the jurisdictional division of labour legislation powers between the Federal and Provincial governments. This could greatly reduce the possibility of establishing a consistent, comprehensive system of participation in all regions and sectors of the economy which may be of vital importance to enterprises with establishments in different jurisdictions. Nevertheless, since the Federal government legislation generally sets the pattern for change, the immediate adoption of a strong Federal policy on worker participation is necessary if it is to be extensively introduced in Canada.

B.   INSTITUTIONAL OBSTACLES

Besides the legal obstacles, three major areas of difference between the West European and Canadian contexts have been identified as potential impediments to the direct application of a German or Dutch-type model in Canada.[58] These differences occur in the focus of collective bargaining, union organization, and labour-management attitudes.

1. The Focus of Collective Bargaining

Collective bargaining in Western Europe has traditionally focussed at the industry or national level, although recently there have been attempts in Germany and the Netherlands to develop a greater trade union presence on the shop floor. Consequently, representative institutions within individual establishments, as the works council, are usually seen to be complementary to, rather than in conflict with, the collective bargaining process even though they represent all employees. In addition to their consultative functions, these institutions are normally responsible for applying the central collective agreement to the establishment and are often utilized as an important source of information for collective bargaining purposes at higher level.

In contrast, the emphasis in Canada is on decentralized, establishment-level bargaining between local union representatives and management; accordingly, there is considerably more union activity at this level. Where many council functions are subsumed under collective agreements, there frequently exist highly developed grievance procedures, and workers may turn to their shop stewards or local union officers for assistance in any matters relating to their jobs.[59] Hence, it is highly probable Canadian unions will adopt a position similar to their British counterparts, opposing the works council on the grounds that it would simply duplicate existing plant bargaining machinery and weaken union influence by creating a separate channel of communication between workers and management. Even if the unions accepted the concept of a works council subject to union involvement, it might be very difficult to establish a system which distinguishes between the consultative and bargaining functions in the usual European manner.[60]

2. Union Organization

The industrial basis of union organization in Western Europe has been cited as a crucial factor in stabilizing the collective bargaining process and facilitating the implementation or extension of worker participation.[61] With one union representing all employees in an industry, collective bargaining structures tend to be well established, which greatly reduces the problems of inter-union jurisdictional disputes and representation arrangements in participative institutions. However, Canadian unions are characteristically organized on a multiplicity of occupational and craft bases. Frequently this results in a number of different unions representing various groups of employees within a given establishment or enterprise. In this context, it may be very difficult to determine an acceptable system of worker representation on company boards and works councils which related the number of representatives to the number of employees as well as accommodating the complex patterns of union representation. For example, in addition to membership size, it may be necessary to consider the unions' relative bargaining powers when establishing the number of representatives to be nominated by each union. A possible situation may occur where a powerful minority union demands an equally powerful position in the new representative institutions.[62] Furthermore, even if an acceptable arrangement was found, there is still a potential danger of internal conflict and polarization arising among the elected delegates leading to inaction and a subsequent loss of confidence in the representative institutions.

3.   Labour-Management Attitudes

Perhaps the greatest potential obstacle to the introduction of worker participation in Canada is labour-management attitudes. The successful development of participation will not depend on enabling legislation but on the willingness of both management and labour to accept cooperation as the basis of their relationship. As a probable result of divergent histories, there appears to be a major difference in attitudes toward labour-management relations in Western Europe and Canada. A striking difference is the attitude towards collective bargaining. While both systems generally have a built-in adversary approach, including the right to strike and lock-out, conflict is much less publicly acceptable as the basis of the industrial relations system in Northern Europe.[63] Normally, labour movements in these countries do not consider the strike as the most effective method for enforcing their demands on management. Instead they tend to regard the power to intervene in daily management affairs as more important for protecting their interests and often seek legislative assistance for achieving their ends.[64] This attitude apparently derives from the post war period when management and labour were committed to national reconstruction requiring close cooperation between the two partners and their respective governments. Moreover, the unions were able to obtain a significant influence over government policy which subsequently encouraged them to seek State support in achieving their objectives. The resulting high degree of union involvement in the economic and political systems has presumably been a main force behind recent trade union pressure for greater worker participation in management decision-making within the individual enterprises.

Conversely, the strong private enterprise philosophy of North America seems to have fostered the adversary approach to labour-management relations where unions regard the right to strike as, ". . . the ultimate weapon, to be used when negotiations fail to provide the wages and working conditions they demand."[65] Tending to view their main function as an external check on entrepreneurial actions, the unions are usually suspicious of any cooperative arrangements which might compromise their independence. Thus, in maintaining an oppositional role to management, North American unions commonly reject the concept of participation in formal decision-making bodies on the principle that they cannot simultaneously protect workers' interests and accept responsibility for management decisions or the success of the enterprise.[66] Moreover, as in the case of the British unions, there is an additional fear such representative institutions could be used to avoid union recognition or weaken their influence. Accordingly, similar to the TUC position, Canadian unions have generally maintained that the primary means of extending workers' influence should be through the continued development of collective bargaining. This view of collective bargaining as being the most effective form of participation at plant level is well expressed by S. H. Slichter who states,[67]

> . . . an important result of the American system of collective bargaining is the sense of participation that it imparts to workers. The many local agreements or local supplementary agreements help create such a feeling. It is true that few workers participate directly in determining their working conditions and and rate of pay, but they belong to organizations that do participate. Hence, the ordinary worker does not feel left out. He knows that important changes cannot occur in markets and technology without their effect on him being considered.

At the same time, there appears to be a growing recognition of certain limitations to collective bargaining in meeting increasing worker demands for greater influence over management decisions. These limitations include: the non-continuous nature of bargaining precluding immediate and direct responses to unforeseen situations; the extent of influence over management decisions - which mainly depend on the union's relative power and militancy; a lack of non-unionized worker representation; and inability to deal with broader social issues.[68] Furthermore, I. Bluestone of the United Automobile Workers of America has observed the collective bargaining process in North America is becoming "overburdened" with too many issues which severely restricts the unions' ability to present new concerns in negotiations. Many of the present issues dealt with in collective bargaining, such as social security arrangements, are provided for under comprehensive legislation in West European countries.[69] He also contends that while North American unions have made considerable progress for their members in quantitative terms by improving working conditions and raising living standards, they have made less progress in qualitative terms, concerned with influencing major social policy issues. Therefore, Bluestone concludes the labour movement must search for new and additional ways of strengthening industrial democracy, possibly incorporating some of the ideas and practices of worker participation existing in Western Europe.[70] The national and international union federations have expressed some interest in ideas concerned with the "democratisation" of the workplace, namely, the need for better communication between workers and management, greater worker involvement in the organization of their tasks, and the elimination of arbitrary managerial authority over work decisions.[71] Consequently, union attitudes may be changing slowly. This would seem to resemble the experience of the British labour movement who were initially opposed to any form of worker participation other than collective bargaining but are now pressing for parity representation on company boards.[72] Whether the Canadian labour movement will make similar demands is still uncertain; however, it may be expected that any new institutional arrangements will be required to operate through trade union machinery.

In accordance with their private enterprise philosophy, North American management tends to resist any arrangements requiring a surrender of their decision-making freedom.[73] Therefore, it may be anticipated that Canadian employers will strongly oppose worker representation on company boards or a works council system with powers beyond mere consultation. It has been observed, Canadian management, ". . . see paralysis as the inevitable result of worker participation in corporate decisions . . . managers see, too, the arrival of the worker director as signalling the end of the coherence, cross-fertilization and easy communication of the present corporate structure."[74] While this current attitude may be primarily the result of inadequate knowledge and experience with worker participation, management resistance may present a formidable obstacle to any immediate introduction of formal representative institutions with decision-making powers.

Still, management appears to be willing to accept the concept of extended worker involvement in the direction of their tasks. Although managers generally accept joint decision-making through collective bargaining, they are beginning to discern certain inherent limitations in the present system as a result of recent experiences with rising levels of labour turnover, absenteeism and industrial conflict. A director of employee research at General Motors has asserted,[75]

> We are on a collision course. We have built institutions which were very effective in their time, but now there are increasing levels of aspirations and different value systems which are pressing against these institutions.

In an attempt to meet new worker demands and value systems, a growing number of managers, particularly in the United States, are initiating experiments mainly concerned with direct forms of employee participation.[76] Even though most of these schemes are established to pursue the pragmatic objectives of greater enterprise efficiency and profits, it has also been perceived they have tended to break up traditional authority relationships and diffuse worker influence throughout the organization.[77] Hence, it would seem successful experience with direct forms of participation is likely to induce a more positive management attitude towards the introduction of worker participation at higher decision-making levels.

The foregoing discussion would imply that any attempt in the near future to establish widely a comprehensive system of worker participation in Canada could encounter several serious obstacles. Therefore, it may be necessary to consider a gradual introduction with government initiating the major changes in public corporations and services while encouraging the adoption of similar arrangements in private industry. As management and labour perceive the benefits and become accustomed to their new relationship, an extensive system of worker participation may become more readily acceptable to both partners.

Notes

[1] Even the European Communities Commission acknowledges the main task of its proposals ". . . is to construct a framework which provides for the objectives to be reached in a way which leaves discretion to the member states as to the precise models which they may adopt." European Communities Commission, *Employee Participation and Company Structure in the European Community*, Supplement 8/75, p.46.

[2] Walker, K.F., *Workers' Participation in Management, an International Perspective*, Geneva, International Institute for Labour Studies, 1972, p.1180.

[3] For a summary of the literature, see Bowleg, J.T., "Final Report on the Seminar," *Workers' Participation*, Paris, OEC, 1975, pp.44-45.

[4] Commission on Industrial Relations, *Worker Participation and Collective Bargaining in Europe*, London, Her Majesty's Stationery Office, 1974, p.31 citing a 1964 study by O. Blume.

[5] Bowleg, *op. cit.*, p.45.

[6] Daniel, W.W., "Report on the discussions at the Seminar," *Prospects for Labour/Management Co-operation in the Enterprise*, Paris, OECD, 1974, pp.13-14.

[7] Bowleg, *op. cit.*, pp.45-46.

[8] Dufty, N.F., *Changes in Labour-Management Relations in the Enterprise*, Paris, OECD, 1975, p.71; Garson, G.D., "Recent Developments in Workers' Participation in Europe," *Self-Management: Economic Liberation of Man*, Vaneck, J., editor, Hammondsworth, Middlesex, Penguin Books Ltd., 1975, p. 183; European Communities Commission, *op. cit.*, p.37.

[9] International Labour Organization, *Participation of Workers in Decisions Within Undertakings*, Labour-Management Series: No. 33, Geneva, International Labour Office, 1969, p.22.

[10] European Communities Commission, *op. cit.*, p.37.

[11] Chotard, Y. "Statement," *Workers' Participation*, Paris, OECD, 1975, p.17; Dufty, *op. cit.*, p.49.

[12] Dufty, *op. cit.*, p.108.

[13] International Labour Organization *Workers Participation in Decisions Within Undertakings*, Labour-Management Series: No. 48, Geneva, International Labour Office, 1974, pp. 48-49; Garson, *op. cit.*, pp.165,176,179,181,183-185.

[14] European Communities Commission, *op. cit.*, pp.37-38.

[15] "Workers on the board," *The Economist*, March 24, 1973, p.67; Bowleg, *op. cit.*, p.53.

[16] Webb, G.H., *Participation - Myth or Reality*, Geneva, International Labour Office, 1970, pp.4-5; Dufty, *op. cit.*, p.72; Bowleg, *op. cit.*, pp.44,61; Daniel, *op. cit.*, p.21.

[17] Bowleg, *op. cit.*, p.50; International Labour Organization, *op. cit.*, p.20.

[18] See Bowleg, *op. cit.*, p.51; Daniel, *op. cit.*, p.17; International Labour Organization, 1969, *op. cit.*, pp.19-20; International Labour Organization, 1974, *op. cit.*, p.43; European Communities Commission, *op. cit.*, pp.38-39; Garson, *op. cit.*, p.165.

[19] Dufty, *op. cit.*, p.50.

[20] International Labour Organization, 1969, *op. cit.*, p.20.

[21] Garson, *op. cit.*, p.184.

[22] In conjunction with his analysis of recent changes in labour-management relations, Dufty has endeavoured to identify the potential consequences of these changes, but he does not attempt an overall evaluation due to the difficulties involved in objective measurement. See Dufty, *op. cit.*, pp.98-121.

[23] Walker, K.J., and de Bellecombe, L.G., *Workers' Participation In Management*, Geneva, International Institute for Labour Studies, 1967, p.30.

24 Walker, K.F., and de Bellecombe, L.G., *op. cit.*, p.30; Bowleg, *op. cit.*, p.51; *The Economist*, March 24, 1973, *op. cit.*, p.67.

25 Commission on Industrial Relations, *op. cit.*, p.18; See also Dufty, *op. cit.*, p.105; Bowleg, *op. cit.*, p.50.

26 Commission on Industrial Relations, *op. cit.*, pp.18,19.

27 Commission on Industrial Relations, *op. cit.*, pp.19,22.

28 Commission on Industrial Relations, *op. cit.*, p.19; Dufty, *op. cit.*, p.105.

29 Commission on Industrial Relations, *op. cit.*, p.19; Bowleg, *op. cit.*, p.51.

30 Commission on Industrial Relations, *op. cit.*, p.22; *The Economist*, March 24, 1973, *op. cit.*, p.66.

31 Dufty, *op. cit.*, p.105.

32 Dufty, *op. cit.*, pp.105-106.

33 Connaghan, C.J., *Partnership or Marriage of Convenience?* Ottawa, Labour Canada, 1976, p.79.

34 Connaghan, *op. cit.*, pp.1-2,79.

35 Commission on Industrial Relations, *op. cit.*, p.31.

36 Dufty, *op. cit.*, p.107.

37 Taken from Balfour, C., *Industrial Relations in the Common Market*, London, Routledge and Kegan Paul Ltd., 1972, p.101.

38 Connaghan, *op. cit.*, p.2.

39 Dufty, *op. cit.*, p.109.

40 See Dufty, *op. cit.*, pp.109-110.

41 For a summary of the studies, see Walker and de Bellecombe, *op. cit.*, pp.32-33; and Dufty, *op. cit.*, p.114.

42 European Communities Commission, *op. cit.*, p.39.

43 European Communities Commission, *op. cit.*, p.39.

44 Walker and de Bellecombe, *op. cit.*, p.33.

45 Commission on Industrial Relations, *op. cit.*, pp.22,128.

46 Commission on Industrial Relations, *op. cit.*, pp.31-32.

47 Commission on Industrial Relations, *op. cit.*, pp.31-32,135.

48 Commission on Industrial Relations, *op. cit.*, p.32; Walker, *op. cit.*, p.1184.

49 Walker and de Bellecombe, *op. cit.*, pp.33,34; Dufty, *op. cit.*, pp.117-118.

50 Walker and de Bellecombe, *op. cit.*, p.33.

51 Walker and de Bellecombe, *op. cit.*, p.33.

52 Walker, *op. cit.*, p.1185.

53 Walker and de Bellecombe, *op. cit.*, p.26.

54 The main analysis to date would seem to be Connaghan's study of the West German system and its relevance to the Canadian situation. See Connaghan, *op. cit.*

55 European Communities Commission, *op. cit.*, p.20.

⁵⁶ For a discussion of the issues involved in this type of company law reform, see Report of a Working Group of the Labour Party Industrial Policy Sub-committee, *The Community and the Company: Reform of Company Law,* London, The Labour Party, 1974, pp.7-17.

⁵⁷ European Communities Commission, *op. cit.,.,* pp.32,40.

⁵⁸ Commission on Industrial Relations, *op. cit.,* pp.123-125, 140-144; Connaghan, *op. cit.,* pp.80-85,91; Daniel, *op. cit.,* p.45.

⁵⁹ Sturmthal, A.F., *Workers' Participation in Management: A Review of United States Experience,* Geneva, International Institute for Labour Studies, 1970, p.167.

⁶⁰ Commission on Industrial Relations, *op. cit.,* pp.140,141.

⁶¹ Connaghan, *op. cit.,* pp.84,91; Commission on Industrial Relations, *op. cit.,* p.141.

⁶² Commission on Industrial Relations, *op. cit.,* p.141.

⁶³ Connaghan, *op. cit.,* p.80; Commission on Industrial Relations, *op. cit.,* p.124.

⁶⁴ Connaghan, *op. cit.,* p.80; Commission on Industrial Relations, *op. cit.,* p.125.

⁶⁵ Connaghan, *op. cit.,* p.80; see also, Dufty, *op. cit.,* p.49.

⁶⁶ Sturmthal, *op. cit.,* p.184; Dufty, *op. cit.,* p.37; International Labour Organization, 1974, *op. cit.,* p.15.

⁶⁷ Sturmthal, *op. cit.,* p.151.

⁶⁸ Bowleg, *op. cit.,* p.57. See also Bluestone, I., "Contribution," *Report on the International Seminar on Workers' Participation in Decisions Within Undertakings,* Geneva, International Labour Office, 1970, pp.153,154.

⁶⁹ Bowleg, *op. cit.,* p.57.

⁷⁰ Bluestone, *op. cit.,* p.156.

⁷¹ International Labour Organization, 1974, *op. cit.,* pp.30-31.

⁷² Bowleg, *op. cit.,* p.47.

⁷³ Bluestone, *op. cit.,* p.156.

⁷⁴ Rumball, D., "Should Workers Help Run Your Company?" *The Financial Post Management,* April 10, 1976, p.13.

⁷⁵ Jenkins, D., *Job Power, Blue and White Collar Democracy,* Garden City, N.Y., Doubleday Books, 1973, p. 199.

⁷⁶ For an analysis of the more significant schemes which have developed in the U.S., see Jenkins, *op. cit.,* pp.188-245.

⁷⁷ Jenkins, *op. cit.,* pp.240-241.

IV

Accommodating Employee Representatives on Boards of Directors

Some major obstacles associated with the introduction of worker participation in Canada have been touched upon in earlier chapters but none was seen as insurmountable. There is, however, one complex problem deserving of close scrutiny, namely, what functions and responsibilities will worker directors have in the board rooms of limited liability companies and what changes, if any, may be required in company law to accommodate employee representatives on boards?

Traditionally, corporate law in Canada gives *shareholders* the right to appoint directors to company boards. At issue are such questions as, who should appoint *employee* directors, and given the legal duties of boards of directors to act in the best interests of the company, can these now be interpreted to mean the best interests of shareholders *and* employees alike?

Canadian corporate law is based on the assumption of private ownership with control of the company residing with the owners in their capacity as shareholders. The law grants shareholders the collective right to participate in the voting to elect directors, thereby giving them a say in the management of the company. They also have the right to share in the company's profits (declared as a dividend by the directors) and in the assets of the company in the event of dissolution. Collectively, shareholders appoint the company's auditors and accept or reject bylaws or articles of association passed by directors in the course of the year. While companies are governed principally by their own bylaws they are also bound by the overriding dictates of corporation law. It should be noted, however, the mere ownership of shares in a company does not automatically give a person the right to intervene in the management of the company.

Almost invariably, shareholders delegate the management of the company to appointed officers. This delegation may be revoked by changing the bylaws or dismissing those appointed. Shareholders' authority to appoint auditors, approve compensatory payments to directors for loss of office, agree to changes in the capital structure and place the company in voluntary liquidation cannot be delegated. In practice, however, unless the shareholders are sufficiently organized, they usually exercise their powers on the advice and initiative of the board of directors.

The order of authority in a company descends as follows: shareholders, directors, executive officers and employees, with the shareholders having the sole right to elect, or remove, directors. Most provinces in Canada insist there be at least three directors, although Alberta, British Columbia, Nova Scotia and Saskatchewan allow for two. When there are more than six directors, they may with the shareholders' permission elect an executive committee from among themselves, with decisions of the committee subject to review by the whole board.

A main characteristic of company law in Canada is its flexibility, keeping interference in the organization of companies to a minimum. True, the legal framework is established but there is little dictation of the structure that limited liability companies must follow.

Legal Duties of Company Directors

Company directors have a number of legal duties and responsibilities in addition to those conferred on them by company bylaws. Fiduciary duties require directors to act in *what they believe to be the best interests of the company they serve*. To achieve this, outside interests that interfere or conflict with corporate responsibilities should be minimized and no unapproved (secret) profit should accrue to directors from holding office. Conditions surrounding insider trading in company shares are well protected by law in contrast to the weak conventions governing confidential corporate information.

The degree of care and skill directors are expected to display in carrying out their duties is far from clear. Before worker directors are appointed to boards the law would need to be clarified for the benefit of all concerned to reduce the possibility of directors inadvertently committing such acts as negligence, misfeasance or fraudulent trading.

Whatever model of worker participation is contemplated in Canada, of particular significance is the corporate requirement that directors act in what they believe to be "the best interests of the company". Theoretically, corporate shareholder and employee interests may be said to coincide. In practice, however, this may not be so, particularly in the short run, when for instance the question of redundancies may arise should a decision be made to substitute capital equipment for labour or to close down a branch plant in the interest of efficiency.

Clearly a new approach is needed requiring directors to consider employees' interests. But in any event, where worker directors (whether union or non-union) are appointed to boards it would be highly unrealistic to expect them to pay sole regard to the best interests of the company to the exclusion of their fellow workers' interests. Given the scope for diversity of values among directors of different economic backgrounds, how far their duties should be specified in law or promulgated in the form of general guidelines becomes a highly controversial question.

Corporate bylaws are the detailed rules governing companies' day-to-day operations. They embody official policy binding the actions and decisions of directors. Power to originate bylaws lies with the directors but they must be confirmed by a majority of the shareholders.

There are three main categories of bylaws,

(1) bylaws of general rules of application or operation,

(2) bylaws authorizing changes to the incorporating document, and

(3) bylaws conferring on directors shareholders' authority to undertake specific transactions not covered under (1) above.

In practice, however, there is great diversity in how companies reach decisions, and in the size, composition and functions of boards of directors. The law may specify the minimum number of directors but it does not state the maximum. Thus the size and composition of boards vary widely, depending on corporate needs, although as a general rule they tend to be proportionate to corporate size.

The Role of the Board

Since the role of a board will tend to correspond with the size, organizational structure and type of product (or service) of a corporation, it is impossible to generalize on the part boards play in corporate decision-making. Evidence suggests the structures of boards may range from those found in small companies, where executive boards of managers may be actively involved in all aspects of the business, to the decentralized groups of large corporations, where types of "holding company" boards appoint top management and allocate funds but delegate day-to-day operations to divisional boards of directors.

Should board-level worker participation be introduced in Canada, some general guidelines may be helpful in establishing which board in a multi-board corporation bears ultimate responsibility for such important matters as the appointment, remuneration and dismissal of top management; company plans, objectives, investment and expenditures; and, within the context of industrial relations, the approval of overall employment policies, including perhaps decisions on extensive layoffs and redundancies. Alternatively, where the boards of large companies delegate considerable responsibility to formal management committees composed of executive directors and divisional managers, the powers of such committees should be specified.

The British White Paper on *Industrial Democracy* while rightly avoiding any firm rules on unitary or two-tier board systems, proposes a two-tier model along Danish lines. Employers will be represented on the top policy board which will be responsible for formulating corporate policy. Seven functions and responsibilities are elaborated in order to avoid the German dilemma whereby employers may delegate important policy decisions to the management board. But the day-to-day running of the enterprise rests with the management board of professionals. Unitary boards are not excluded if the parties prefer this method of accommodating employee representatives.[1]

Evidence regarding the role of non-executive directors on boards and in corporate decision-making is hard to come by but the general opinion is they serve primarily as custodians of shareholders' interests and as independent advisors on general corporate policies. They may also be appointed in order to lend prestige to companies and because of their special knowledge of, and influence in, the world of labour, management and government.

Analysis of Canadian corporate structures has led some observers to conclude they cannot be categorized. Theoretically, however, it may be agreed these tend to be unitary, although in many instances the dichotomy between theory and practice may lead large corporations to adopt what is in effect a *two-tier system* (remotely akin to some West European models) with ill-defined powers, where the functions of supervision and management are shared at different levels of the enterprise. Technically the power of initiative over decision-making may be retained by a main board.

The important issue here is not the structure of boards of directors but rather the locus, magnitude and importance of decision-making functions in the company in the event employee representatives are called upon to participate. At which level and on which board or committee would worker directors have the opportunity to express views on, and have a say in, decisions that affect them? Moreover, crucial to the controversy surrounding worker participation is the question *whether employee involvement in the decision-making process can best be achieved within the existing framework of Canadian company law or through a revised two-tier system, along West German lines, of a supervisory and a management board, each with carefully defined powers,* or even by adopting a modified Danish model, which recognizes overlapping jurisdictions between supervisory boards of directors and management.[2]

Insofar as company law and practice in Canada are tolerably consistent with or may be modified to accommodate the principles of *effective* employee representation on boards of directors, it may be better to opt as the British have done to seek accommodation within the present flexible system rather than impose rigid or inappropriate legal formulae that may prevent companies from devising structures best suited to their purposes. This is not to suggest the law remain unclarified regarding the functions and responsibilities of boards and their relationship to shareholders, management and employees. Introducing worker participation at the board-room level without clarifying the present system could mean employee representatives on boards have the illusion of influencing decisions that in effect are made either by shareholders or management committees. Moreover, it would be unfair to ask management to accept worker directors on boards without defining the role and functions of such newly constituted bodies. The authority of management and their responsibility to these boards must be formally spelled out along with any restrictions on their discretion to take executive action in the absence of policy guidelines.

It will be clear from the foregoing that if it is agreed that industrial democracy could be served in Canada by accepting the principle of worker participation in managerial decision making, then in addition to attitudinal changes some ideological changes in company law and practice would be called for to accommodate those employee representatives who are elected to serve on boards of directors as *direct representatives* of their fellow employees, and who are free from dismissal at the whims of the shareholders. Two problems arise in obtaining corporate efficiency in light of this new relationship between labour and capital: firstly, how best to balance the interests of employees and shareholders so the former can make a genuine and useful input into corporate decisions while the latter retain a say in how their investments in the company are managed, and secondly, how to achieve these desirable objectives with minimum legal and government intervention.

Board Structure and Functions

Given the interest in, and success attributed to, the West German system of worker participation, it is inevitable that debate will centre on the merits of that country's *statutory* two-tier board structure compared with the existing unitary North American system, which, with appropriate modifications, may fit a Canadian or U.S. model of worker participation. The distinction between the two systems is at times clouded in view of the emergence of a *de facto* two-tier system in large companies in Canada, but it should be borne in mind that in West Germany the law is unequivocal in establishing two tiers of corporate control, the board of management and the supervisory board, on which employees are represented. The functions of each are detailed in law, with supervisory boards consisting of equal employee representation required in all companies employing 2000 or more workers.

Although supervisory boards have no managerial functions, they nevertheless possess important supervisory powers over management. They appoint management boards, scrutinize company accounts and accept responsibility for all major policy decisions. Their powers of intervention are, however, circumscribed in that they cannot arbitrarily dismiss members of boards of management without cause before the expiration of term, and in that their veto rights over certain transactions may be overruled if management can obtain the support of 75 per cent of shareholders. *Both boards are responsible to the company, not the shareholders.*

The substitution of a modified form of the West German two-tier statutory system for a unitary one might lead to instances where two different and separate corporate procedures could prevail. This could happen if some small companies with say fewer than a specified number of employees were not required to adopt worker participation or where unions were unable to agree on the principle of the system (and therefore did not request it) or failed to obtain sufficient support for it from their members.

It has been argued the introduction of a two-tier system in Canada need not follow the *formal* West German approach. It is thought that an *informal* system comparable to the more flexible Danish model could become operationally functional within a North American context (given a high degree of goodwill). But before Canadians adopt even the less formal Danish approach a number of aspects deserve careful consideration. For instance, there may be demands that the separation of supervisory board responsibility for strategic policy and supervision of management from those of managerial decision-making be legally specified along with the respective functions of each board. To attempt to codify these functions and impose unfamiliar regulations on the highly flexible and pragmatic Canadian system might be detrimental to managerial efficiency. Interposing separate managerial and supervisory functions bearing little resemblance to the corporate structure which had evolved over the life of the company could be disruptive and might ultimately become inoperable. Evidence from France suggests the introduction of an *optional* two-tier system in that country has had only limited success, due primarily to friction and conflict between supervisory boards on the one hand and management boards, which tend to be controlled by shareholders, on the other. It is important to note the West German system of two-tier boards evolved over decades, long before worker participation was considered, in response to shareholders' demands they be allowed closer supervision of management. The corporate structure there thus developed within this legal framework before representation became an issue. To attempt to graft that kind of inflexible two-tier system on to an entrenched North American system might frustrate the endeavour to improve industrial relations, and inadvertently enlarge managerial prerogatives by its mere inflexibility. For these reasons, the less restrictive Danish two-tier system seems more acceptable within a Canadian or U.S. context. It permits supervisory boards to intervene in managerial board functions while clearly recognizing overlapping jurisdictions. It falls well short of allowing the top board to intervene in day-to-day management functions, however. Boards of directors in

Denmark (including employee representatives) are responsible for the management of companies and take part in management via management boards. Members of boards of management operate according to guidelines and instructions from the boards of directors, *subject to certain provisions designed to promote efficient decision-making within each enterprise.* The intent is to ensure that supervisory boards are strong enough to influence managerial decisions while still allowing managers to manage. Moreover, having employee representation on top boards of a two-tier system avoids the problem of a unitary system, which may give worker directors too much contact with day-to-day management.

Irrespective of whether a two-tier or a unitary system of employee representation is followed in Canada, if worker directors are to have a voice in company affairs, the role and functions of boards of directors will need to be clarified so that final decisions on major questions of policy are not taken outside of boardrooms or overruled at shareholders' meetings. It would therefore be desirable to specify more precisely in law at what point corporate decision-making powers would rest with boards of directors, under what circumstances the latter would be allowed to delegate authority to top management and which kinds of boardroom proposals shareholders would be given the right to accept or reject.

There are several important functions normally considered the sole responsibility of boards of directors. These include the dissolution of the company, changes in the articles of association, decisions re payment of dividends, modifications in the company's capital structure and the sale of assets, disposition or allocation of resources, and all aspects of top management's terms of employment.

Reserving these functions for consideration by directors would not call for any substantive changes in the current procedures of most companies. However, there are implicit changes relating to functions attributed to boards, which, when specified, might restrict management's right (but not initiative) to act unilaterally where ultimate responsibility resides with boards. Such constraints might not represent major changes for many companies in Canada since most important corporate matters are invariably referred to boards of directors for final decision. The significance of codifying these board functions lies in protecting employee representatives from dictatorial attempts by management to by-pass their boards.

Acceptance of the above suggestions need not negate the power of boards to delegate authority to management. Delegation is essential for corporate efficiency. Prior agreement on whether an important issue such as collective bargaining will be undertaken at the shop steward-middle management or top-management levels or dealt with initially in the boardroom would need to be reached. The expectation is, however, that in order to accommodate employee representatives on boards, the onus would rest with newly formed boards to decide whether matters previously delegated entirely to management are to be discussed in boardrooms before decisions to delegate are made. No doubt difficulties would arise in establishing guidelines on which policies and matters are considered of sufficient importance for board review and decision and which properly belong to management. Eschewing the codified West German approach in favour of flexibility would permit each company to devise its own participation techniques best suited to the circumstances.

Role of Shareholders

The relationship between boards of directors and shareholders would be modified under the above proposals as the traditional synonymity of shareholders and company ownership changes. The power of shareholders to overrule board decisions on matters important to employees and management would no longer be unrestricted. Worker participation implies a partnership between capital and labour (rather than an adverse relationship), with management acting as the go-between yet serving to promote the interests of all parties. To illustrate, not only shareholders but also employees are affected by changes in a company's articles of association, capital structure, payment of dividends, sale of assets or dissolution of the business. Instead of decisions on these matters being an exclusive prerogative of shareholders they would now require consultation with boards, since it is improbable that employee representatives (particularly if their constituents are represented by strong unions) would find the status quo acceptable. But these proposed changes may not in fact be as drastic as they seem. Current practice among progressive companies is for all concerned to consult with each other on most important corporate matters. Formalizing this consultative mechanism by specifying how power to take decisions between boards and shareholders will be distributed would be advantageous. Most companies in Canada include in their articles of association provisions empowering the directors to originate bylaws (subject to confirmation by a majority of shareholders) and to declare dividends. Minor amendments would bring the law into line with reality. Shareholders could retain veto power over board decisions but they would be unable to take an unusual step such as initiating major policy changes without prior approval of a board. It is worth noting that in many states in the U.S. shareholders do not possess the sole right to decide certain important matters of corporate structure or policy; proposals emanating from boards of directors are approved or vetoed or require approval of both before a decision is agreed.

Worker participation would of course reduce shareholders' power of control over board appointments in that a proportion of these appointments would now be made by the employees. Apart from this change, the power of shareholders to appoint directors would remain substantially the same.

With employee representatives on boards of directors, it would not be unreasonable for both representatives and constituents to expect some statement of basic duties required. Whether these duties should initially appear as guidelines that may subsequently be codified is an open question. Flexibility and perhaps a period of experimentation are called for while worker directors gain experience. All directors should have the same unequivocally stated duties and responsibilities. This does not preclude worker directors from taking into account the interests of their constituents, however, although it should be made explicit that voting in a particular way on trade union instructions would be inimical to the cause of industrial democracy. By striving for the objectives of corporate efficiency and economic viability, directors would advance the interests of all concerned.

Confidentiality

Employee representatives would no doubt be expected to report back to their constituents. Directors' reports, audits and other pertinent documents available for shareholders' inspection should therefore be made available to employees. European experience indicates these are essential steps for the success of worker participation and that one of the major advantages of representation lies in the more general acceptability by workers of decisions that have been reached by boards that included employee representatives. Reporting back inevitably raises the question of confidentiality and whether legal restraints should be placed on the right of worker directors to disclose classified information to their colleagues. Most West European jurisdictions now make it mandatory for companies to disclose information to trade unions in the belief that the resulting benefits of increasing confidence and understanding between management and workers far outweigh the potential cost in terms of breaches of real or assumed confidential information. The rules of confidentiality can always be invoked when warranted while still providing for the release of confidential information where relevant to collective bargaining. Evidence from West Germany and Sweden suggests the question of confidentiality, considered highly contentious when experiments with employee representation were first introduced, turned out to be insignificant. Any system of industrial relations is not without its difficulties. Worker participation is no exception. Would it be too much to hope that many of the anticipated obstacles may turn out to be illusory were worker participation to be introduced in Canada?

Notes

[1] Cmnd 7231, *Industrial Democracy,* H.M.S.O., London, 1978, p.16.

[2] The British may opt for the Danish model. Proposals are for a joint representation committee (JRC) to be set up in each company employing more than 500 workers. After 3 or 4 years experience with a JRC workers in large firms (2000 or more employees) will have the legal right to board-level representation. If this cannot be agreed voluntarily, employees may appoint one third of the directors to the policy board (given a two-tier system) or to the existing unitary board. See, Cmnd 7231, *op. cit.,* p.16.

V

Influence of Participation on Collective Bargaining

The Role of the Government

In the previous chapters one recurring principle was the concept and successful implementation of worker participation resting on the awareness of common interest among employers and employees, but nevertheless government involvement is paramount. The present role of government in the prevention and settlement of industrial disputes in the *private* sector in Canada is still highly contentious, despite the fact both federal and provincial governments have been involved for decades. There are some who argue there is too much unwarranted government intervention in labour-management functions in the private enterprise sectors while others assert it is only by increased government involvement that the near monopoly powers of big unions and corporations can be properly regulated to serve the general good.[1] This controversy on the role of government has intensified in the past few years because of intervention in the bargaining process by the Anti-Inflation Board (AIB) and the proposals and counterproposals for more formalized "economic planning" and "social contracts" to be agreed by government, unions and management. It is unlikely therefore the controversy will lessen in the years ahead when those who are quite genuinely concerned about the current adversative state of labour-management relations begin to take a serious look at the relative merits and demerits of worker participation. Important questions will arise over the precise role governments should play were such an innovation to be implemented in Canada. And while much will depend on the model (or models) of worker participation adopted in order to shed light on the probable nature of the controversy (and its possible resolution) it may be advantageous to take a brief look at the background and unique features of *current* Canadian labour legislation *applicable in the private sector* and then to examine those influences, such as the collective bargaining process, which will undoubtedly be modified under this fresh approach.

Since the rules and conventions of collective bargaining are normally circumscribed within the legal framework any future developments or reforms in industrial relations policy in Canada - whether they be simply a modification of present collective bargaining procedures or adoption of innovations such as worker participation - will generally have to be undertaken within this framework. In light of comments throughout this study, readers can speculate for themselves how a policy of worker participation can be grafted to the existing system without drastic change and yet fundamentally alter the traditional adversary approach inherent in today's collective bargaining procedures followed in private enterprise.

Present Industrial Relations Policy

In Canada, industrial relations public policy is controlled by both the federal and provincial governments. Each jurisdiction has its own sphere of operations derived from the British North American Act (B.N.A. Act) and court interpretations of this important constitutional document. The division of powers between the federal government and the provinces is contained principally in Sections 91 and 92 of the B.N.A. Act of 1867. Although neither of these sections makes specific reference to a labour relations function, Section 92 does state that provincial legislatures shall have the exclusive right to make laws relating to "property and civil rights" in the province. Inasmuch as labour relations legislation is mainly concerned with the exercise, or restraint on the exercise, of civil rights, and since such exercise of restraint has an indirect effect on property, it follows that *provincial legislatures have primary jurisdiction over labour relations*. This fact has been established over past decades by several important judicial decisions[2] and is of paramount importance should an attempt be made to introduce some form of worker participation throughout Canada. Although the power to enact labour relations legislation lies chiefly with the provinces, it is not in fact absolute. There are three instances where the federal government has overriding authority to pass labour legislation. Firstly, it may legislate in regard to persons engaged in works and undertakings assigned to its jurisdiction under Section 91 of the B.N.A. Act. Secondly, Section 92 makes provision for the federal government to legislate with respect to transport and communication agencies extending beyond the limits of a single province and local works or undertakings declared by the Canadian Parliament to be for the general advantage of Canada or for the advantage of two or more provinces. Finally, during a national emergency the federal Parliament may extend its legislative authority to the extent it considers necessary to preserve "peace, order and good government" within the nation. And while extensive use of this power has been confined to wartime, in the absence of constitutional amendments, it is probably the Section under which the federal and provincial governments could agree to introduce worker participation.

There are certain features of Canadian federalism that are particularly significant with respect to development of a national labour policy. The executive of the federal government has the power to disallow any Act passed by a provincial legislature, whether or not the Act deals with subjects falling within the legislative field exclusively assigned to the provinces. The federal government can instruct the Lieutenant Governor to withhold his assent from provincial bills if it sees fit. Thus, although the central government cannot itself legislate upon provincial subjects, it can effectively prevent the provincial legislature from doing so. Of further significance is the restriction that the Parliament of Canada and the provincial legislatures may not *directly* delegate their legislative powers from one to the other. Each level of government may exercise only the powers given to it by the B.N.A. Act. And while the federal government alone possesses the constitutional authority to impose, for example, a mandatory nation-wide policy on worker participation, the provinces could effectively negate such a measure unless they agreed in advance to indirectly delegate authority to a common agency operated by the federal government on the nation's behalf.

Labour relations legislation has been passed by the federal government and all the provinces. Obstacles to the broadening of it to include worker participation provisions are not insurmountable. Current legislation serves four main objectives.

1) It provides for the certification of trade unions as the bargaining agents of employees.

2) For the purpose of negotiating collective agreements, it requires employers to engage in collective bargaining with certified bargaining agents.

3) Where disputes arise during the negotiation of new collective agreements, it serves to prevent strikes or lockouts until a conciliation procedure has been complied with.

4) During the life of collective agreements strikes or lockouts are prohibited. Such disputes are to be settled by arbitration or otherwise without a work stoppage.

Canadian governments have extended their influence into the four main areas where disputes between labour and management may arise. These areas are:

a)   union certification,

b)   union recognition,

c)   bargaining collectively over an agreement, and

d)   grievances over the interpretation of the agreement.

To prevent or settle disputes arising over union certification, union recognition or the negotiation of new collective agreements, quasi-judicial labour relations boards (possessing exceptional powers to administer the law) and conciliation systems have been established. For disputes arising from the interpretation of existing agreements grievance procedures have been established with provision for one person or three party, *ad hoc,* boards of arbitration. The belief is the introduction of worker participation would narrow, substantially, areas of disagreement under item (c) above; that area which remains the most contentious under our present system.

Strictly speaking, the present Canadian system of industrial relations is not one, but a multiplicity of systems, one for each province and one for the federal government, and each is constitutionally free to develop independently. However, despite this legislative freedom in the eleven jurisdictions, the actual labour relations policies in force in each province bear a resemblance to each other and to federal laws. Unifying influences have, in the past at any rate, tended to outweigh the pressures for differentiation. For example, most provinces require that when the status of the applicant union meets the statutory requirement and the appropriate bargaining unit has been determined by the board (of industrial relations) the union must then satisfy the board that it has the majority of the employees in the unit as members in good standing. But before the union is granted certification for the employees in that unit, representation votes may be conducted under the supervision of the board. All jurisdictions require employers to recognize and negotiate with the union(s) once certified for a unit, and almost all provide for some form of state intervention by way of the assistance of a conciliation officer when direct bargaining between the parties fails to produce an agreement. If a conciliation officer is unable to induce the parties to settle the legislation may offer a discretionary form of government assistance by means of a conciliation board. Until recently strikes were illegal until after the board had reported. Now, boards are only appointed if the minister considers it advisable or the conciliation officers recommend it. Should a grievance, i.e., a difference of opinion, arise between an employee and management over interpretation or application of an existing agreement, most statutes have provisions governing the final settlement of such "rights" disputes and some set out the steps both the union and management must follow to resolve it. Work stoppages, i.e. strikes and lockouts, are prohibited over issues involving certification, recognition and grievances, and they are generally illegal until after the conciliation procedure has been met.

Given the influence of many United States international unions on their Canadian affiliates, it is pertinent to contrast the patterns of development in Canadian and American industrial relations,[3] since authorities in the United States likewise are contemplating a move towards worker participation. American emphasis was placed on controlling private power possessed by employers so as to guarantee the freedom of workers to exercise their rights. It was not concerned with specific disputes about terms and conditions of employment. American law clearly assumed the road to industrial peace was paved with collective bargaining. The role of government was therefore to make this process compulsory and then let it work by itself, with only an incidental assist from mediation where that might be useful and the parties might be willing to accept it. There was no restraint on the strike. The National Labor Relations Board (NLRB) was set up by the U.S. Federal Government as a permanent piece of government machinery to administer the legislation and was given extensive authority to do so. In contrast, *the Canadian approach was to intervene in the actual dispute itself,* conditional on proof that a strike or lockout would probably take place. Support for collective bargaining was incidental to the conciliation and investigation of specific disputes. Even with the introduction of the principle that employers in Canada should be legally obliged to bargain collectively with the union certified by law for the appropriate unit of employees, emphasis on government intervention remained strong. It will thus be seen that Canadian legislation reflects two views with respect to state intervention into industrial disputes, the accommodative and the normative. The first approach seeks to help the parties reach a mutually determined agreement, whereas the second tends to substitute third party judgment for the judgment of the parties themselves. While American policy at the federal level is strongly accommodative, being careful to place restraints on the normative approach, Canadian law is ambivalent on the question of the approach to conciliation. *Indeed, the most prominent characteristic of Canadian labour law has come to be its high degree of government intervention and compulsion;* acceptance of this fact in the past leads some observers to assert that it should be easier here than in the U.S. for government to introduce a model of worker participation operationally acceptable within a Canadian conciliation context and which would, in part, remove many of the controversial aspects of contemporary conciliation practices.

The Role of Conciliation

Some of the mandatory aspects of Canadian labour legislation have been widely and persistently criticized and further government involvement is unlikely to prove no exception. But gradually, over time, most unions and employers have come to accept certain aspects of it, such as the grievance procedure, as advantageous, although unions occasionally question the inflexible certification and representation requirements and the practice of governments supervising votes on such issues. And while these requirements may unintentionally serve to delay the parties from commencing collective bargaining it is the conciliation requirement which has come in for the severest criticism on the ground that once negotiations have begun (but the parties cannot reach agreement) it tends to delay the settlement of disputes by prohibiting a strike until after the conciliation officer has attempted to settle the issue. Given this requirement and strike prohibition settlement is said to be delayed rather than encouraged because the threat of a work-stoppage cannot be used at that juncture.

There are indications the introduction of worker participation in Canada may be opposed on the grounds it would contribute little more than the existing conciliation system was intended to achieve. It is probably true that successful conciliation, whether voluntary or compulsory, should lead to the establishment of stable and constructive collective bargaining relationships between labour and management, which in turn should assist in limiting the number of work stoppages. It has even been suggested that successful conciliation is a self-liquidating process, leading to a situation where labour and management can negotiate collective agreements without the assistance of a third party. That this sequence of desirable events has not happened in Canada is a matter of profound disappointment to the policy makers (who placed such faith in the efficacy of conciliation) as well as to those who have to comply with it.

The Canadian system, as previously indicated, has been criticized on the ground that it does not foster sound state-free and vigorous collective bargaining; in fact some observers contend that where government techniques of dispute settlement obstruct or impede collective bargaining, they probably increase the amount of conflict, rather than improve labour-management relations. This may happen if the disputants take such a firm stand during negotiations that neither can retract without losing face. Therefore, strikes occurring after prolonged conciliation may be more difficult to settle. It has been argued by some the only achievement of the Canadian system has been to postpone some strikes by enforcing a delay between the breakdown of private negotiations and the beginning of a work stoppage. Officials of some large trade unions and corporations have expressed the opinion that where the services of conciliation officers are interfaced at negotiations such a degree of intervention has not helped the parties to develop a mature, self-reliant, attitude towards collective bargaining. It has tended to foster apathy among the disputants during the early stages of negotiation. Responding to this opinion, most governments have now made conciliation boards optional and strengthened the role of conciliation officers in the procedure, by increasing their status, prestige and authority to assist them in discharging their duties. As a result of this action, the long delays in passing disputes through conciliation have been reduced and a source of much irritation to unions and employers removed. Despite the removal of the conciliation board requirement *ad hoc* boards may still be established on request or if the authorities feel they are warranted; spokesmen for some of the large and powerful trade unions, such as the steel and auto workers, maintain that blanket application of compulsory conciliation for all types of industrial dispute without regard to the nature or economic importance of the industry, the size of the firm or the number of employees involved, merely delays real negotiations until after the legal formalities have been complied with. Indiscriminate use of the conciliation requirement may lower its value in the eyes of labour and management, fostering the opinion that it is merely an annoying, intermediate step. Opinion appears to be moving to the view that the use of government conciliation services might best be offered on a *voluntary* basis except where pending disputes seriously threaten the general public interest, in which case government would presumably retain the right to intervene by prohibiting a work stoppage and appointing a mediation or fact-finding commission to resolve the issue.

One premise is the basic weakness of compulsory conciliation as now practised in Canada lies not so much in the conciliation process itself as in the legal suspension of the work stoppages during the conciliation period. Some authorities assert the positive role of the strike has been overlooked particularly where it serves the purpose of forcing the parties to come to an agreement by posing a threat of losses to both sides in a dispute. This traditional view of collective bargaining has been well-expressed by the authors of the federal Task Force on Labour Relations,[4]

> . . . collective bargaining is designed to resolve conflict through conflict, or at least through the threat of conflict. It is an adversary system in which two basic issues must be resolved: how available revenue is to be divided, and how the clash between management's drive for productive efficiency and the workers' quest for job, income and psychic security are to be reconciled. Other major differences, including personality conflicts, may appear from time to time but normally they prove subsidiary to these two overriding issues.

It is further argued that since Canadian labour relations policy tends to delay the threat of conflict the result may be to weaken the process of bargaining and delay settlements. And while few, if any, of those involved want a work-stoppage, over-emphasis on the harmful effects and failure to recognize the significance of its role in collective bargaining presents the danger that existing public policy may weaken the evolution of labour relations and confine the process to pre-determined channels.

During the past decade such traditional views of collective bargaining have been questioned. Adherence to a system which served well in periods of relative price *and* wage stability is no longer considered appropriate. Greater flexibility might lead to innovation and experimentation in the development of sound labour-management relations through worker participation.

But in evaluating the Canadian system of mandatory conciliation, its positive effects must not be overlooked; indeed the skills acquired by conciliators may prove to be readily transferable (with minimum retraining) should worker participation be introduced. An experienced conciliator who may have helped parties without previous bargaining experience to reach their first agreement with relatively little difficulty may continue to render similar valuable services in participatory negotiations. He could, if requested, serve as a kind of *ex officio* chairman for the parties to foster a spirit of compromise and if necessary act as a go-between, thus enabling labour, management and shareholders to make concessions without loss of face. The tact and objectivity of a conciliation officer may thus serve as a tempering influence on the three parties involved by inducing them to meet any new legal requirement introduced and, above all, to negotiate in the more enlightened atmosphere which worker participation implies. The possibility of utilizing these useful attributes to make the fresher more challenging approach of worker participation a reality should not be neglected. With appropriate guidelines, conciliation divisions across the country could provide the staff to assist the parties in this new venture.

Government Supervised Voting

Before concluding this short review of the chief legislative requirements for collective bargaining in Canada today, it is worth mentioning that since worker participation will require the election of employees to councils or boards, voting procedures will become important. Some governments currently undertake to supervise workers' votes on such questions as union certification, recognition and conciliation awards and, as in the case of Alberta, strikes. At issue therefore are the questions, should government be involved in the election of employees where, (a) no union is involved and, (b) the establishment is only partially unionized and, (c) the plant is fully unionized. Many voting practices were initially introduced in times of emergency in respose to the feeling among the public and to some extent employers, that workers (even when members of a trade union) needed some protection from union leaders. Will this view prevail in the case of (b) and perhaps (c) above? The belief that in the absence of some kind of supervision the rights of workers, for instance, to belong or not to belong to a union, might be abrogated and that employees may be induced to vote contrary to their feeling is still strong. Most union leaders do not accept this view and in (b) and (c) above will perhaps justifiably consider any control over voting as a restriction of their right to manage their own affairs. Even under worker participation the union must be concerned with strategy of its long-term relations with management and shareholders and presumably is entitled to argue that it be allowed some influence on decisions of signed up and prospective members, and permitted to discourage workers from considering their individual interests, perhaps at the expense of their wider responsibilities to the group. Despite these contentious possibilities the mere fact that it now is customary for governments to require votes be taken on certain issues may prove salutory should worker participation be introduced. The election of employees to work councils or supervisory boards would be examples.

Provincial legislation varies on matters of voting where industrial relations are involved; some require majority authorization from employees *entitled to vote,* other than a clear majority of those who cast ballots. Union officials argue where the former regulation is followed, abstention is unfairly interpreted as a negative vote. But retention of supervision of voting seems to be based mainly on the assumption that union leaders generally favour actions contrary to those workers would opt to follow. Those jurisdictions intending to set and perhaps scrutinize voting procedure will have to be quite specific regarding their requirements. Evidence from Britain suggests some unions plan to resist any intervention in their voting procedures, despite indications they may sometimes need external scrutiny to restrain their more militant and youthful members. Certain control provisions are almost invariably written into union constitutions, requiring, for instance, that such important issues as strikes can only be authorized by the international or national head office after union leaders have obtained at least majority vote in the local. Extension of such provisions to cover employee elections, for example, to work councils or supervisory boards, might prevent unnecessary controversy at the establishment level. But serious consideration should be given to the mandatory use of postal ballots at public expense. Irrespective of the type of worker participation followed, union executives will probably still wish to restrain the power of the rank-and-file to keep them from making irresponsible decisions. To illustrate, inquiry into the course of events when a strike vote is taken at the local's meetings tends to support the union leader's statements that they often have a hard fight restraining an impetuous membership from advocating strikes, and inducing them to accept a conciliator's award or terms offered by the employer which their negotiators considered favourable; and while there is every reason to believe the course of events will be different when employees are called upon to make decisions in light of more complete knowledge of company affairs, safeguards may still be desirable.

From this brief and very general summary of some of the salient requirements currently prevailing in many industrial relations jurisdictions in Canada, the controversial features of the legislation (particularly those designed to outlaw or reduce strikes and promote settlements) have been highlighted in the belief that the introduction of some form of worker participation will remove many of the controversial features. It was stated initially that while the Canadian constitution grants to the provinces primary jurisdiction over the major portion of labour legislation, *in practice a pattern of leadership by the federal government has tended to be established over past decades.* This fact has significant implications for the introduction of new innovations such as worker participation or any other reforms to industrial relations legislation which may be considered in Canada. The onus and responsibility for change probably still rests with the federal government. As already noted, the Canadian system of industrial relations is characterized by a high degree of government intervention intended to induce both unions and management to abide by the rules of the game. This fact, in spite of the controversy surrounding it and the frequent expressions of dissatisfaction from the disputant's side, may ultimately prove beneficial. The experience gained should enable employers and unions to put their knowledge to constructive use. Appraisal of current policy has been generally critical in that some of those (especially the unions) who are required to operate under it assert it does not foster the establishment of stable and constructive collective bargaining relationships between employees and employers. The system may have been reasonably successful in the past in promoting sound labour-management relations; today, the question is frequently asked, *can a system of industrial relations designed to cope with economic and social conditions mainly in the first half of this century* (when arbitrary decisions on the part of employers could give rise to insecurity of income and poor working conditions were dominant) *adequately serve the needs of a well-educated and skilled labour force in an economy subject to increasingly rapid technological change, irregular economic growth,*

and particularly the complex, unresolved, problem of inflation?
Moreover, with the granting of collective bargaining rights to a
substantial number of workers in the public and quasi-public sectors,
can similar legislation serve to regulate the rights and responsibilities
of employees in the public sector (where the employer is the
government) as those in the private sector? But before summarizing the
feasibility of reforming existing industrial relations procedures in the
private sector to accommodate such changes as worker participation, it
is necessary to consider the *conventional* tactics of collective
bargaining (and the part played by that weapon of last resort - the strike
- in resolving industrial conflict in order to aid us in assessing more
clearly the anticipated changes in labour-management negotiations
which worker participation may bring.

The Conventional Bargaining Process

In a present day context, to bargain collectively means to negotiate
in good faith with a view to the conclusion of a collective agreement, or
the revision or renewal of an existing collective agreement which
jointly determines and administers wage and non-wage benefits and
the terms of employment between a union representing the workers and
the employer or representatives of a group of employers. Both the
negotiation of a collective agreement and the administration and
interpretation of its terms as applied to daily problems come within the
scope of this definition. With the introduction of worker participation,
this definition will be broadened considerably to accommodate some
or all of the items listed in chapter one under both direct and indirect
forms of participation. The essential difference is a redistribution of
power in labours' favour whereby employees may influence decisions
previously taken at the managerial/board of directors levels. A
prerequisite to collective bargaining is, of course, employer
recognition of the union which has been certified as the representative
of the workers in the appropriate unit, and this requirement remains
under worker participation. Previously, once certification had been
obtained an employer, while legally bound to recognize *and* at least go
through the motions of bargaining with the union, was not obliged to
reach an agreement. Failure to reach agreement is less unlikely under
worker participation.

Conventional collective bargaining emphasizes economic issues
and areas of potential conflict between the two parties and also stresses
the continuous relationships between labour and management and the

compromises implicit in defining their respective rights and duties. The end product of negotiations is a collective agreement — a body of working rules and regulations accepted by both labour and management. These rules and regulations are administered by both the establishment and the union, and are interpreted through the quasi-judicial process of the grievance procedure through which an aggrieved worker may appeal to union and management representatives and finally to a third party (an arbitrator or arbitration board) for a decision that is final and binding. Collective agreements negotiated through the bargaining procedure are subjected to renewal and amendment at the end of a specified period of time. It is not anticipated any redefinition would be required here except to note that negotiations may involve shareholders if the corporate structure does not delegate sole authority to management.

The federal government and the relevant authorities of most provinces have been exerting an increasing influence both on the procedures of collective bargaining and on the determination of the terms and conditions of employment as exemplified recently in the powers and functions of the Anti Inflation Board. Over the years governments have sought to protect not only the interests of those workers who wish to bargain collectively, but also the interests of the non-union worker and the public. And while the resulting legislation lays down the rules within which collective bargaining may function, it does not, apart from exceptional circumstances, take away the power of management and unions to arrange their own contracts subject to any temporary limitations imposed by an agency such as the Anti Inflation Board. Aside from this latter reservation which may in the present context be viewed as temporary, ''free'' collective bargaining continues to exist in Canada. Again, modifications to these aspects of traditional collective bargaining may be slight except the usual adversary elements in negotiations are likely to be diminished. Much will depend on where the locus of decision-making power rests, that is, with management or company directors.

Worker participation in common with collective bargaining is a process of voluntary agreement requiring mutual accommodation and effort by the parties to find a common middle ground. Agreement is reached whenever the cost of agreeing for one of the parties is less than the cost of disagreeing. Conflict is still implicit in the process but where there is a genuine effort to find an accommodation with employee involvement in decision-making the probability of conflict reaching the work-stoppage point is lessened considerably. Differences of opinion still have to be resolved. Thus as with the conventional approach to contract negotiations by making disagreement more costly than agreement, or agreement less costly than disagreement, the parties (which now include spokesmen for shareholders or their delegates) agree to the proposed terms. The fact that as long as the union and company continue in existence some bargain has to be reached, and while eventually this leads each party to put maximum pressure on the other, the ultimate decision is more likely to be the rational one rather than second best. Irrespective of the industrial relations system followed, an employer may be willing to pay all that is necessary to keep his present workers and to lure additional workers if required but he is not likely to pay more than this. Under worker participation actual negotiations at the bargaining table should differ from the conventional approach. The latter, as is well known, requires each party to keep from the other knowledge of the rate on which he would actually be willing to settle until he can explore on what issues and at what rate his bargaining opponent is likely to accommodate him. There is bluff and blow in the process and a negotiator cannot always guess how firm is the position of his opponent without occasionally calling his bluff. Consequently, even when the employer is ready to pay what is required and the union may be able to win no more than its members would have obtained anyway, the convention surrounding collective bargaining seems to require this strategy which may inadvertently lead to strike action. Normally unrealistic demands are wittled down in reaching an agreement at the bargaining table, but militant union members or company officers may repudiate the settlement and force their negotiators into a strike, despite the fact a fair and reasonable agreement has been reached. There is of course, no guarantee that where worker participation is agreed that the "games strategy of negotiations" will be changed substantially, old customs and practices are hard to break, but the belief is in the fresh atmosphere of frankness and consultation, those involved will see the futility of the old approach in light of the new commonality of interests.

Conventionally, in disputes involving public services, in the parties' determination to reach an agreement and avoid an arbitrary *ad hoc* (legislated) settlement, either the employer or the union may be forced to exclude some important innovation such as a productivity clause from the bargaining process. Under these circumstances, inasmuch as a settlement is merely a postponement of bargaining over basic issues, post-negotiation activity often concentrates on minimizing the real cost of unresolved problems. *It is not surprising, therefore, that conventional collective bargaining as a method of settling industrial disputes particularly in public utilities* (such as rail or air transport and communications) *or service industries* (such as schools or hospitals) *or in industries where redundancy is a problem, has been criticized for its excessive cost in terms of time and resources wasted.* And as a means of determining employee's compensation, that is, wages and non-wage benefits, in an era of both unacceptably high inflation *and* unemployment the rationale behind it is increasingly under attack. It is, of course, debatable if the addition of worker participation principles to public sector negotiations will resolve the problems outlined. Perhaps the best that can be hoped for is for the reason which will prevail in the private sector to be transmitted to the public sector as a tempering influence.

Despite the latter comments, there are certain benefits to be derived, in theory at least, from private sector collective bargaining (which sociologists and psychologists emphasize must not be overlooked) that should be enhanced by worker participation. Ideally, *the direct and indirect consequence is to bring about more consideration for the freedom, dignity and worth of workers in modern industrial society.* Sound collective bargaining provides a drainage channel for specific dissatisfactions and frustrations which workers experience on the job and it enhances the dignity and worth of labourers in their role as factors of production, thereby humanizing an essentially impersonal price system. Even if, as some economic evidence suggests, income levels of workers are not substantially influenced by the process, the establishing of *money* wages through bargaining, is thought to give workers a feeling that blind and relentless economic forces are being properly tempered by human forces. Collective bargaining allows for flexibility that fits well into the vast differences existing between industries, regions and periods of time, but the gap between theory and practice is vast. This idealistic process will unquestionably be improved by more objective consideration of facts, via employee participation in decision-making which should result in genuine effort to link wages to productivity and more effective selection and better training of employee representatives. This is not to deny that the conventional approach to collective bargaining did not have within it the potential for creative innovations and the promise of broadening participation to include all those workers affected by the decisions. The ideal bargaining process both creates the machinery and provides the rationale for endorsement of capitalism by employers, shareholders, labour leaders and workers alike. And indeed it may be argued these features make collective bargaining well worth saving. But this can only be done by widening its scope and improving the system to accommodate innovative changes.

However, despite the theoretical advantages claimed for collective bargaining, Canadian labour, management and shareholders sooner or later will be faced with the choice of cooperating voluntarily on some form of innovative changes or be compelled to do so by government and the tenor of public opinion. Unless a more constructive and realistic approach is taken towards wage and non-wage determination at the establishment level, in both the private *and* public sectors, eliminating unnecessary conflict , free collective bargaining will ultimately, in the opinion of many labour relations specialists, be restricted through enforcement of more permanent forms of wage-price controls or by compulsory arbitration, or by some other form of government intervention. Labour and employers (with an assist from government and academics) must together find cures for the defects and abuses of collective bargaining as it is now practiced in all sectors of the economy and make constructive efforts to solve problems within an enlarged framework if they are not prepared to accept the alternative of increasing and decisive government intervention. *If either labour or management, or owners of capital insists that free enterprise permits them to be indifferent to socially determined objectives, then it is inevitable that society will move against free enterprise to curtail it in society's own interests.*

Other Approaches to Collective Bargaining

Readers may well argue the foregoing assessment of the contemporary Canadian industrial relations system is too pessimistic and that innovative changes may remedy its defects, thereby avoiding the need to introduce worker participation which may be anathema to some employers and unions. Response to this argument is that other approaches to collective bargaining have not achieved the desired results. In fact, it remains questionable whether collective bargaining in its present form, even if conducted without a work-stoppage, is adequate for the needs of our modern technological society. Prior to the introduction of wage-price controls, the evidence seemed to indicate clearly some negotiated terms (fully acceptable to both unions and management) could, at the same time, be obstructive to the attainment of major national objectives. The basic difficulty seems to be the dimensions of the economic aspects of employer-employee relations are not fully perceived or certainly not publicly admitted by many important leaders in both the private and public sectors. How are the vital goals of national economic planning to be achieved while the strengths of the free enterprise system are maintained, and the prospects for innovation within the existing framework of collective bargaining limited by tacit adherence to the status quo? This is a critical matter requiring purposeful cooperation between the public and private sectors of the economy if an adequate answer is to be found. A number of trends have developed in this area and have been tried in Canada with varying degrees of success. For instance, the achievements of joint consultation and continuous bargaining are noteworthy and in many cases imply steps towards greater employee involvement in work-place decisions which affect them. But the evidence is most of these trends have been temporary, stop-gap measures which only in rare instances have reached to the heart of the problem which afflicts industrial relations. The reasons for this lack of success are complex but without *genuine* participation in decision-making and a redistribution of power in favour of employees permanent improvement is improbable.

The above comments need not imply where innovations have been introduced that they should now be abandoned in favour of worker participation. Rather than being mutually exclusive they are more likely to be reinforcing. For instance, there are many useful features of continuous bargaining which could be retained to fit in with the consultative approach suggested.

CONTINUOUS BARGAINING

Most current departures from conventional bargaining in Canada are along the lines of continuous bargaining which readers will note bears a strong resemblance to the methods implicit in worker participation. Conventional bargaining has not proved to be very effective outside the traditional wage, hours and conditions of work issues. Complex problems posed by increasing foreign and domestic competition, automation and the dichotomy between employment and wage levels cannot be solved in the superheated atmosphere of the usual bargaining sessions. Sound, well-thought-out and well-executed solutions are not likely to result from crisis bargaining toward an arbitrary strike deadline. For this reason, progressive companies have adopted the alternative of discussing particularly difficult problems in joint, year-round meetings, removed from the publicity and pressures of normal bargaining. They have found that continuous joint consultation may make bargaining on complex issues easier and more fruitful. As unions increase their role as agents for social improvement and economic growth there emerges a greater community of interest between management and labour and a greater degree of mutual confidence and co-operation. This technique requires employers to coordinate the technical and human aspects of industrial management, combining good plant relations with efficient production by displaying responsibility to their workers as well as to their shareholders. The kind of expression and refinement which has been brought to the management of corporate assets in the last few decades is needed in this approach to the management of human assets. Conscious effort at career planning by the individual, his union and his employer is required.

Although many variations of this co-operative technique have been adopted, all involve the same basic element, continuous bargaining during the life of a collective agreement and a closer working relationship between the employer and the union. Ideally, advance consultation and planning between labour and management should start with the first indication of impending change and should be continuous. Some negotiating committees include neutral outside representatives skilled in labour relations, in addition to the union and company officials; the neutral members, in some instances, being granted powers of mediation should formal negotiations become deadlocked. Establishments which successfully follow some variant of continuous bargaining should have no difficulty making the transition to worker participation. The difference would be in the *formalized redistribution of power* to employees under the latter system.

EARLY BARGAINING

In many instances diluted forms of continuous bargaining are also used. As a compromise between continuous discussions and the orthodox practice of exploring mutual problems only after formal negotiations have begun, "early bargaining" has been introduced. This involves setting up joint union-management committees to study specified problems a few weeks or months before contract negotiations open. Although agreement on particular solutions may not be reached, the objective is to map out the factual dimensions of complex issues for the negotiators. Bilateral fact-finding helps provide a neutral framework within which controversies based on conflicting interests may be resolved. Difficulties may arise, however, if committee studies tend to postpone decisions and arouse the suspicion of union members. This is particularly significant in view of the current tendency for the rank-and-file to revolt against what they consider to be an increasingly authoritarian attitude of the unions, the latter resulting from their growth and bigness. However, without a contractual obligation on the part of employers to provide joint committees with relevant information and give them a say in the making of decisions which involve employees, early bargaining may lack substance and be used as mere window-dressing by management as a sop to weaken union leadership. There is only scant evidence of successful early bargaining in Canada.

Government Participation

Crucial to any discussion of worker participation is the debate over the need for, and extent of, government involvement to promote it. Evidence from other countries supports the view its introduction is unlikely to be successful if participation is voluntary. On the other hand, should the requirement be mandatory in establishments of a certain size or within certain industries how will provisions be enforced?

As mentioned earlier, there is considerable divergency of views as to the proper role of government in employer-employee relations. These views are worth clarifying in order to shed light on the pending controversy. It may be argued the government can build a collective bargaining environment better suited to modern technological needs by less compulsion and more voluntarism, greater consultative help and re-examination of all laws and administrative procedures, so as to build more flexibility and mobility into private relationships. The government's role in such a case would be limited to providing the basic rules within which labour and management are free to seek their own solution. They would refrain from passing legislation on matters properly the subject of collective bargaining. If they become involved in tripartism, it is felt governments may inhibit true co-operation. Their primary responsibility would thus be limited to the use of monetary and fiscal policy to ensure adequate expansion of job opportunities. Such government policy, it is argued, would ease collective bargaining over work rules and protection of jobs and leave to it the task of finding solutions to problems of adjustment arising from technological change.

Supporters of this philosophy feel it is best not to legislate which areas are, or are not, subject to negotiation. Accordingly they would argue the wisest public policy, so far as statutory duty to bargain is concerned, is that expressed by Canada's Minister of Labour at the time the Industrial Relations and Disputes Investigation Act was passed in 1948,[5]

> . . . only such regulation of employer and employee activities in their industrial relationship as is considered necessary for the protection of the public interest is incorporated in the legislation. The main responsibility is left with labour and management for the settlement between them of their problems, the negotiation of collective agreements and the administration of such agreements . . . the most constructive public policies toward labour-management relations will not make the mistake of confusing the mere avoidance of open but orderly strike with the advancement of public or private interest . . . it is not government's job to maintain peace at all costs. And if there must be curbs on the right to strike, . . . then those curbs should be seen for what they are: a high price paid to avoid the assumed higher price of an interruption of production.

Under a policy of restricted government intervention, provision of government services which bargaining parties are free to accept or reject would be possible. The Canada Manpower Consultative Service (CMCS) of the federal Department of Manpower and Immigration has been designed with this function in mind. It encourages advance planning for change in private employment situations, joint union-management study of problems and provision for supplementary government assistance on a voluntary basis. Through publicly financed incentives for study, formulation of technological adjustment plans, and relocation and retraining of displaced workers, the Service offers positive inducements to provinces, employers and unions to adapt to technological change or manpower planning needs incurred during industrial expansion. Its recently broadened terms of reference enables it to study such issues as job satisfaction, job enrichment, job barriers and problems of the work environment. It also provides consultative services to private parties (both unions and management) to aid them in settling their own problems.[6]

Contrasted with this policy of ''discretionary'' government intervention into employer-employee relations is one which would invite government participation through extensive legislation and tripartite negotiations. *The critical question is how much government intervention is required to protect the public interest.* This depends largely on how effectively labour and management discharge their bargaining responsibilities in fields where work stoppages and uneconomic contracts inflict their primary damage on the community.

It is argued when all the people have to suffer through the willfulness or ineptitude of economic power blocs it is an affirmation, not a denial, of democracy to provide effective government machinery for breaking deadlocks. On this basis, it is felt that government is quite legitimately a third force at the bargaining table. Accordingly, in modern industrial societies collective bargaining cannot remain free of all intervention by government. Indeed, in the absence of voluntary restraint or the widespread move towards worker participation, if collective bargaining stands any chance of meeting the challenge of the future, it may ultimately become necessary for government representatives to form a permanent third party of interest in negotiations. Their function would be to represent the public interest, preventing collusion that would be injurious to public welfare and coordinating private and public planning. It therefore seems likely that if collective bargaining is to be preserved, decisions will sooner or later have to be made at the national level for national application. No group in society can be allowed unilaterally to make all decisions. It will become necessary for employers, employees and shareholders at the establishment level to co-operate to plan jointly economic activity and make joint decisions about economic and social goals and the means of achieving them. It is inevitable that some loss of traditional autonomy by all groups will be involved.

There is an additional aspect to this problem. The burdens of training and retraining, of job finding and job making, cannot be borne solely by a particular company and union whose resources and horizons are necessarily limited. To promote economic growth and preserve economic stability, it is essential for the government to offer assistance in this area. It may also be practical for the government to establish voluntary guidelines for appropriate ranges of economic settlements which are considered vital to the national interest. Following this line of reasoning, it becomes the function of government to exercise its influence and exert strong pressure to make collective bargaining agreements conform to the broader interests of the public. Supporters of this policy feel such government participation would not impair the constructive consequences of collective bargaining, provided compulsory legislation is not the basis for such action. But the crucial issue is, should voluntary restraints fail what other options are available to society short of mandatory wage-price controls similar to the recent Anti Inflation Board regulations?

Whether or not current legislation is adequate for the role assigned to government by this latter type of policy is debatable. With increasing frequency governments have intervened through *ad hoc* legislation to forestall work stoppages in vital industries by substituting a process of compulsory arbitration for collective bargaining. The temporary success of such actions gradually gave way to voluntary restraints in the early 1970's culminating in the Anti Inflation Board of 1975. If collective bargaining is to be retained, any statutory solution ought to maximize pressures for bargaining in, for example, the more enlightened atmosphere which worker participation provides while safeguarding the public against potentially harmful work-stoppages. Failure to recognize this need could mean that bargaining may cease to exist in these situations. And while an element of flexibility is needed in the settlement of disputes, to preserve the vitality of the bargaining process observers of the successful application of worker participation procedures emphasise that more acceptable solutions are invariably reached under these procedures than with the conventional form of collective bargaining.

Industrial Relations Council

Can legislation be relied upon to guarantee the high level of responsibility, integrity, democracy and social consciousness expected from labour, management and owners of capital? It is apparent that no formula or law is going to bring an end to all employer-employee conflict. It is the spirit in which the problems are tackled and the regulations imposed that is significant. This is the prime justification for advocating the widespread introduction of worker participation. However, while improved labour-management relations cannot be brought about exclusively through the compulsory adoption of worker participation, it is also apparent the use of this system would serve to deter either party from precipitous acts such as unwarranted strikes or lockouts, and also fulfill an educative role by publicly declaring expected standards of conduct. Therefore, worker participation legislation directed toward the shaping of the destiny of employees in their dealings with employers should be enacted with the assistance and participation of those most directly concerned — unions, management and shareholders.

A national council for social and economic planning has been proposed, in which labour, management and public officials (and perhaps informed members of the academic community) could meet regularly to discuss matters of common interest and to advise and consult on policies regarding legislation. Evolving from this council would be proposals on the course of future policy which would be aired for discussion. It is expected regulations based on such proposals would more effectively command the obedience of all concerned because of the kind of tacit precommitment to legislative policy by all interested parties. Would it be too much to expect such a council to broaden its horizons to consider the innovation of worker participation which has had such success elsewhere? The present failure of labour relations legislation in Canada to keep pace with social and political change is credited to the fact such legislation is currently the product of vigorous and belligerent lobbying by each side for a new law with which to club the other into submission rather than the outcome of a tripartite consultative mechanism whereby programs introduced are subject to the ongoing scrutiny of the consultative body.

Work Stoppages

The mere fact that worker participation may be introduced in Canada does not automatically imply that work stoppages thereafter will be eliminated. *Such a view would be totally unrealistic.* A reasonable expectation would be an improved climate of industrial relations and therefore a lessening of disagreement over contract negotiations - the main area of contention in contemporary industrial relations. What follows below are some brief observations on this important issue.

Generally speaking, the work stoppage has been eliminated as an instrument of bargaining power over issues involving union certification and recognition and in that class of disputes known as grievances, these disputes being referred to arbitration if they cannot be settled between the parties directly. The challenge facing employers, employees and shareholders is to lessen the incidence of *disputes involving the negotiation of collective agreements which remain the major area of conflict* (wages being the major issue). Controversies over job security (particularly when technological change is involved) and the right of employers to use manpower more efficiently often served under conventional bargaining to increase the volume of industrial conflict. Such issues are usually resolved successfully under worker participation as evidenced in the West German coal mining industry. But in a growing number of industries, and even within the public sector, the increasing substitution of capital equipment for labour is now operating to reduce the efficacy of the strike to the point where it is of little value to the unions as an instrument of bargaining power. Once production has become highly automated, a small number of supervisors or non-strikers may be able to maintain operations without strikebreakers. Likewise, sustained over-capacity and large inventories, particularly in some segments of the mining industry, have reduced the effectiveness of the strike. In these instances a shut down in mining operations may continue for a long time before either the employers or the consumers feel any economic pressure. As a result, the character of several recent strikes, for example, the post office, ranging from work to rule to rotating strikes have tended to take on political overtones. To this extent, they have become more a device to embarrass government by attracting public attention in the workers' favour and less a device to damage employers by economic deprivation. Whether unions are achieving positive results in this respect might well be debated, however. Indications of growing public frustration may cause a loss of sympathy for the protesting workers and lead to demands for further government intervention.

In many cases strikers are now often enabled to withstand a work-stoppage of long duration without serious hardship through benefits received from accumulated strike funds, or through welfare payments made to the dependents. Employers have similarly turned to strike insurance funds, and even to the hiring of professional strikebreakers, to soften the economic impact of a work-stoppage. In some instances a strike may even be welcomed as a means of reducing accumulated inventory. Thus the economic pressure on the struck employer to come to terms with the union may be materially reduced. The work-stoppage can go on longer without as much hardship as formerly to either strikers or employers while damage to the economy may increase. Affluence and strategy have made it possible, or perhaps even necessary, for the parties to wait each other out longer. Consequently, work-stoppages often inflict greater punishment on the public than on the warring parties. From the community's standpoint, *the essential question is whether the conventional approach to collective bargaining is an adequate instrument for protecting the public interest,* not just the interests of organized labour and employers. As strikes become cheaper for the disputing parties they become costlier for the public. Although it is argued that work stoppages are the price that society must pay for the privilege of decentralizing economic decision-making and placing it in the hands of the people who have to live under those decisions, opinion is moving towards the view that some strikes (particularly in the quasi-public sector) are an unnecessary price which the public is paying for inefficient and irresponsible negotiation. It is not only the unions which have at times used power for their own advantage. Employers too, in the private sector, on some occasions, have imposed unwarranted hardship and inconvenience on communities.

In light of Canada's record of work-stoppages relative to other industrial countries, the need to eliminate, or at least diminish, the cause of strikes is becoming paramount. The fact that strikes can and do occur not only within large and strategic industries in the private sector but also in the public sector represents a serious economic loss. Industrial machinery is so expensive and industrial processes and services so interdependent that a single prolonged work-stoppage can affect seriously the growth of the nation's economy, even to the point of creating a crisis of confidence in the foreign exchange rate of the nation's currency. Many industries perform services of such vital public importance that the government feels compelled to intervene to prevent strike activity. As indicated earlier, *work-stoppages in Canada today arise primarily from disputes involving the terms of the agreement itself,* of which wages and other non-wage cost items form the major obstacles. Under our present system settlement is dependent on the play of relative bargaining powers. Where long strikes do occur, the balance of economic power is often so even that neither can bring the other to its knees no matter how long the tie-up lasts. The result is an eventual accommodation on terms virtually identical with those an arbitrator or fact-finding commission might have been expected to recommend without any suspension of work. Thus, the work-stoppage seems to have become an anachronistic device in a society which seeks to rely more heavily on rational social processes to complement its rationalized production processes. Therefore perpetuation of the conventional collective bargaining system "designed to resolve conflict through conflict" is no longer acceptable to a growing but vocal proportion of the electorate. To find a reasonable alternative to the work stoppage by which people can help decide the terms and conditions under which they work, would be to improve the democratic process, not destroy it. To repeat, the contention is that the time has come when all those directly involved in industrial relations should seriously consider the innovative alternative of worker participation as a means of reducing conflict.

With the growing public intolerance of the work stoppage and, in many instances, its diminishing effectiveness as a bargaining instrument, the need is apparent for a better and less costly means of motivating agreement if a free trade union movement and collective bargaining are to be preserved. It has been noted that as the strike's economic impact on the disputing parties themselves diminishes, so does the effectiveness of collective bargaining - with the burden transferred to the general public. This is not to deny that unless work-stoppages remain as a possibility, then no genuine collective bargaining is likely to occur. Therefore, any alternative means of inducing a settlement must retain two basic elements inherent in the work-stoppage threat. The outcome must be uncertain and each party must have some means of making disagreement on its terms costly to the other party. Without effective bargaining power there would be no reason for either union or management to concede what the other wants. These basic elements are retained under the proposed system of worker participation; the essential difference being the "adversary approach" ceases to be the accepted negotiating strategy and is replaced by the concept of equality in bargaining and commonality of interests stemming from the shift in the locus of power towards employees.

Controlling work stoppages implies government intervention. The "arsenal of weapons" approach has frequently been suggested in that it retains the element of uncertainty. Under this scheme, if labour and management could not resolve their own dispute they could be certain of government intervention, but the government would be free to employ whichever of a number of devices was most suited to the particular occasion. Since the parties to the dispute could not predict how they would be affected by government intervention there would be some inducement to reach agreement on their own terms. Among the devices available to the government are mediation, the injunction, seizure of the corporation, fact-finding commissions, and compulsory arbitration. *This approach fails to permit each party to impose a cost of disagreeing on the other's terms, however,* and in part explains why few of these devices have been tried. It has been suggested this weakness might be overcome by making compulsory arbitration costly. If unable to settle their own problems, labour and management would submit their dispute to a neutral board whose services would be made about as expensive as a strike might be if it were allowed. Either the same charge could be made to each party or a sliding scale could be introduced which would base the union's cost on the number of members involved in the strike and the company's cost on its assets, with some maximum being set in both cases. Under this procedure, the workers would stay on the job and receive full pay for their work, and the company would continue to produce and receive full return for what it sold. Once arbitration was begun, the length of the proceedings would depend on the parties. Only by reaching agreement with each other could the hearing be brought to a close. Under this procedure, uncertainty as to the outcome would be preserved and it would leave each of the parties with bargaining power which it could bring to bear on the other so that the basic collective bargaining process would not be undermined by needlessly resorting to other devices.

Other proposals include alternate types of action such as the non-stoppage, graduated and/or attenuated strike. The non-stoppage strike would allow the enterprise to continue operating but both sides would be obliged to contribute an amount equal to some given percentage of the total wage bill to a special social projects fund. In a graduated strike employees would be allowed to cut their scheduled hours of work by an agreed proportion and suffer a corressponding loss of pay. The effect on the public in this case might be less drastic than an outright and sudden work-stoppage. Attenuated strikes would be subject to statutory time limits at the end of which period compulsory arbitration would impose a settlement on the disputants. *Most of the above proposals have, of course, been advanced in recent years solely as interim measures. Some have been tried with varying degrees of success while others are viewed as impractical. But none gets to the heart of the matter; any long term attempt at reducing the record of industrial disputes must ultimately aim at correcting the anomalies inherent in a system designed to cope with problems from an earlier era.*

It is for these reasons that all those directly involved in industrial relations, whether they be unions, employers, shareholders or government should weight seriously the merits of the existing procedures against the advantages of the proposed alternative. No matter how Canada's industrial relations record is viewed whether in terms of man days lost per thousand paid workers or average duration of work-stoppages, the country has fared badly relative to most other industrial countries. Our approach to the resolution of industrial conflict is clearly unsatisfactory in that it is not achieving the results intended. Whether the fault arises from the constitutional division of powers under the BNA Act (which, it will be recalled, gives provincial legislatures primary jurisdiction over labour relations) or whether it lies with legal procedures, union and management structures or neglect of the pervasive power of economic (and social) forces (or all of these), is impossible to say, but the evidence is clear there is urgent need for improvement. The argument advanced by many union and management leaders that the present system of industrial relations in Canada must be retained, usually rests on the belief that it worked well in the past and can work again. But this rationale suggests a lack of initiative in considering the possibility of viable alternatives particularly those which have been successfully adopted elsewhere. We live in a dynamic world the essence of which is change, yet students of industrial relations observe how the parties most closely concerned while arguing vociferously for vague, unspecified reforms, fight tenaciously to retain the *status quo,* for fear that change might give an unforeseen advantage to the other. Fresh innovative ideas are needed to improve the system.

The Need for Reform

The effectiveness of the conventional approach to wage determination through collective bargaining has long been the subject of investigation and controversy in Canada. Most students of the system assert it is in urgent need of reform, since it is seriously deficient. Many constructive suggestions for improving the efficacy of the system have been made, but few of these ideas have been accepted by either unions or management. The argument that unfettered collective bargaining buttresses the free play of market forces to provide an effective and rational system of income distribution is suspect in view of the strong monopolistic powers possessed by several industries and unions. It is highly improbable countervailing power was ever as effective as its proponents believed and the chances of introducing greater competitiveness in wage determination between different groups of workers - even if society considered it desirable - is likely to remain an impossible dream. The problem of introducing greater equity into the distribution of income among the Canadian workforce, given the power structure of giant national and multi-national corporations on the one hand and economically powerful trade unions on the other, at first sight appears incapable of solution. There is widespread support for the view that strong unions, bargaining with monopolistic employers, can obtain substantial money wage increases which raise unit labour cost and which are subsequently passed on to consumers in the shape of price increases. Less well organized groups of workers may therefore suffer a relative loss of income. The latter injustice, coupled with the frequent inconveniences of industrial strife, was bound—sooner or later—to cause workers in the non-union or less strongly unionized sectors to take action in their own defence.

Attempts on the part of a growing number of both professional and administrative employees have been widespread to organize themselves into effective bargaining units with a view to safeguarding their economic and social interests. If this trend continues, the problems associated with the conventional approach to collective bargaining (as a means of determining both wage and non-wage benefits) are likely to be intensified in the future. Work-stoppages may increase in number and duration as several government welfare programs unintentionally provide workers' families with the means to withstand the economic hardship of strike. If this analysis is correct a crucial question arises: can the Canadian economy bear the strain of industrial unrest, as well as the political, economic and social instability which may accompany it?

There is abundant evidence from Britain, Sweden and elsewhere that newly organized groups in the labour force - whether they be civil servants, policemen or army officers - are prepared to back up their demands by going on strike when they feel that their earnings, relative to other comparable groups, have fallen behind or are threatened by the activities of other more militant workgroups. Deprivation of relative status within the hierarchy of earnings, it would appear, is now sufficient inducement for ordinarily responsible work groups to act with uncharacteristic militancy without any apparent regard for the wider interests of society. *To argue as many union leaders and employers do that these issues can be resolved through existing conventional collective bargaining procedures without third party intervention to look after the public interest is to ignore the economic and social realities of life. In fact, adherence to existing procedures appears likely to intensify and perpetuate this relative sense of injustice and aggravate labour-management strife to the point where government will have no alternative but to further intervene in a manner and to a degree hitherto unknown in democratic countries - except in times of war.* Thus, if society is not prepared to accept a high degree of state control of earnings in the future, it appears inevitable that before long employers and employees must move in the direction of a more objective and rational means of income determination rather than relying on conventional methods of collective bargaining based on a crude adversary system which frequently degenerates into bitter industrial conflict.

Research findings in the behavioural sciences indicate reform is long overdue in managerial and union attitudes, particularly in the way wage rates and non-wage benefits are determined via conventional collective bargaining. With business growing increasingly complex and technologically oriented, a systematic approach to the problem of wage and salary payments (including non-wage benefits) is needed. As social values change and levels of education rise, a more youthful and vociferous workforce is demanding that union leaders and employers take its views into account in collective bargaining negotiations by giving it a greater say in the running of its workplaces. This demand by employees to be consulted on many matters affecting their welfare is now a socially recognized right. *The right of workers to share in the profits of the enterprise and the right to joint determination of certain aspects of corporate policy is now widely accepted by most progressive employers within the common market countries of Europe, as well as in such socially oriented countries as Yugoslavia.*

Failure on the part of management, unions and shareholders to seek ways and means to improve the climate of industrial relations will result in federal and provincial governments (through the use of new regulatory agencies or *ad hoc* legislation) involving themselves in some form of mandatory incomes policy or in the termination of industrial conflicts where the disputing parties seem unwilling to settle. But such agencies - whatever their nature and no matter how well devised they may be - cannot foster industrial peace where a spirit of compromise and good faith is lacking. *It is for this reason that a new participatory approach to industrial relations is advocated whereby increases in industrial efficiency are emphasised in return for which the gains accruing are shared after consultation between employees, shareholders and industry.* In order to achieve industrial efficiency it is implied that labour will agree to accept new working methods in exchange for gains in pay and working conditions. The efficacy of this approach which is in essence a more formalized version of efficiency bargaining, has long been recognised in Europe and is gaining ground among progressive employers in North America. It goes far beyond the bounds of labour-management relations as conventionally practised in that not only are wages and non-wage benefits jointly determined but all those policies affecting employees are agreed to in advance. With joint participation at all stages of decision making and in the creation of the agreement, a continuing spirit of constructive collaboration is obtained rather than the more usual adversary situation implicit in the old approach and which ordinarily leads to reluctant compromises on issues such as managerial prerogatives and union's rights. Under this new approach management, labour and shareholder representatives define the plant-wide changes they are seeking and those involved respond with modifications and/or trade-offs until a suitable compromise is reached. A successful agreement will specify the rationale underlying the changes agreed. Ideally, such changes should be carefully costed with the benefits accruing to those involved in the establishment weighed against the costs.

Limitations of time do not permit detailed discussion of this important innovation in industrial relations. But the evidence suggests that it offers an attractive and acceptable way of ridding any establishment of inefficiencies by providing a realistic means of combining efficiency with economic advances for employees (including management) and gains for shareholders. Unfortunately, negotiations may be complicated and slow, given the probability of tripartite involvement, and while there are certain basic steps and common principles which may be followed, it is still an art form where the human element is generally dominant. In the final analysis, however, it is workers and not machines which produce, thus is must be recognized that job satisfaction (and some degree of job security) is essential if productivity is to be raised. The introduction of some form of worker participation acceptable within a Canadian context would go a long way to improving the system.

Notes

1 F.R. Anton, *Role of Government in settlement of Industrial Disputes* (Don Mills, Ontario: CCH Canadian Limited, 1962), pp.16-17. Throughout this chapter the analysis applies only to establishments in the private sector. An end result of worker participation should be to bring about more stable prices and incomes which in turn are transmitted to the *public* sectors where in any event worker participation is not unknown (e.g. academic institutions).

2 Federal Department of Labour, *Judicial Proceedings respecting Constitutional validity of Industrial Disputes Investigation Act of 1907* (Ottawa: Queen's Printer, 1925), pp.8-41.

3 F.R. Anton, *op. cit.,* pp.12-13.

4 *Task Force on Labour Relations* (Queen's Printer, Ottawa, 1969).

5 Quoted by Dr. John R. Coleman in an address, the text of which appeared in *Labour Gazette,* Vol. LXIV, No. 11, November, 1964, p.957.

6 A new industrial relations service to assist labour and management in the development of more constructive relationships has also been introduced by the Canada Department of Labour. Evidence suggests that unions and management want to improve their relations via consultation, fact-finding and problem-solving especially in the latter stages of negotiations. The service is administered by the Union-Management Services Branch.

Bibliography

There are extensive bibliographies on workers' participation (industrial democracy) with one of the most comprehensive being that by Roland van Holle entitled *Workers' Participation in Management 1970-1974* published by the International Institute for Labour Studies, Geneva. Canadian readers should refer to back issues of *The Labour Gazette* for informative and provocative articles which have appeared on this subject during the past three years.

Adams, R. and Rummel, C. *Workers' Participation in West Germany: Impact on the Workers, the Enterprise and the Trade Union.* McMaster University, Faculty of Business Research, no. 117, 1976.

Adizes, Ichak. *Industrial Democracy: Yugoslav Style.* New York: Free Press, 1971.

Anton, F.R.D. *Wages and Productivity: The New Equation.* Toronto: Copp-Clark, 1969.

Asplund, Christer. *Some Aspects of Workers' Participation.* Brussels: International Confederation of Free Trade Unions, 1972.

_____ , "What Can Be Done to Advance Labour/Management Cooperation? A Trade Union View Looking to the Future," in *Prospects For Labour Management Cooperation in the Enterprise.* OECD, Paris, 1974.

Balfour, C. *Industrial Relations in the Common Market.* London: Routledge & Kegan Paul Ltd., 1972.

Barbash, Jack, "American Unionism from Protest to Going Concern," paper presented at a meeting on December 27, 1967 of the Association for Evolutionary Economics (mimeo).

Barkin, S., "Labour Participation: A Way to Industrial Democracy," *Relations Industrielles.* 33(3), 1978.

Barry-Braunthal, Thomas, "Labor vs. Management in Europe," *European Community*. May, 1972, pp. 14-16.

Batstone, E., and Davies, P.L. *Industrial Democracy: European Experience*. London: HMSO, 1976.

Bellecombe, G. *Workers' Participation in Management in France: The Basic Problems*. International Institute for Labour Studies, Bulletin No. 6, 1970, p. 85.

Blanpain, Roger, "Provision of Information," Unpublished paper, University of Leuven, July 15, 1974.

Bluestone, Irving, "Worker Participation in Decision Making," paper presented at the Institute for Policy Studies, Washington, D.C., March, 1973.

Blumberg, Paul. *Industrial Democracy: The Sociology of Participation*. New York: Shocken, 1969; English ed., 1968.

Bok, Derek C., and Dunlop, John T. *Labour and the American Community*. New York: Simon and Schuster, 1970.

Brannen, P., Batstone, E., Fatchett, D., and White, P. *The Worker Directors*. London: Hutchinson, 1976.

British Institute of Management: Working Party Report. *Front Line Management*. London: 1976.

_____. *The Board of Directors*. Management Survey Report No. 10, London: 1972.

_____. *Participation, Democracy and Control*. London: 1979.

Burditt, A.R., "France," in *Worker Participation: The European Experience*. Coventry and District Engineering Employers Association, Coventry: 1974.

Business Europe, "United Kingdom Embraces Co-determination in Surprising Turnabout," *Business Europe*. Vol. XIII, No. 13, March, 1973, p. 100.

_____, "Industrial Democracy in Western Europe: The New Challenge To Managers," *Business Europe*, March 15, 1974, pp. 81-82.

Butteriss, M. *Job Enrichment and Employee Participation - A Study*. Institute of Personnel Management, London: 1971.

Canadian Pulp and Paper Association. *Views of the Pulp and Paper Industry Concerning Labour Management Relations in Canada*. Montreal: 1977.

Carby-Hall, J.R. *Worker Participation in Europe*. London: Croom-Helm, 1977.

Clarke, R.O., Fatchett, D.J., and Roberts, B.C. *Workers' Participation in Management in Britain*. London: Heinemann, 1972.

Coates, K., and Topham, A. *Industrial Democracy in Great Britain.* London: MacGibbon and Kee, 1968.

Confederation of British Industry. *The Responsibilities of the British Company.* London: CBI, 1973.

Connaghan, C.J. *Partnership or Marriage of Convenience?* Ottawa: Labour Canada, 1976.

Cox, R.W., Walker, K.R., and de Bellecombe, L.G. *Workers' Participation in Management.* Geneva: International Institute for Labour Studies, 1967.

Crispo, J. *Industrial Democracy in Western Europe.* Toronto: McGraw-Hill Ryerson, 1978.

Cummings, T.G. and Malloy, E.S. *Improving Productivity and the Quality of Work Life.* New York: Praeger, 1977.

Derber, Milton. *The American Idea of Industrial Democracy, 1865-1965.* Urbana, Ill.: University of Illinois Press, 1970.

Dodge, W., ET. AL. (eds). *Industrial Relations in Canada: Towards a Better Understanding.* Ottawa: Conference Board of Canada, 1978.

Emery, F.E., and Thorsrud, Elner. *Form and Content in Industrial Democracy.* London: Tavistock, 1969; original, 1964.

European Communities Commission. *Employee Participation and Company Structure.* Luxembourg: 1975.

Fatchett, D. *Industrial Democracy: Prospects After Bullock.* London: Institute of Personnel Management, 1977.

Flanders, A., Pomeranz, R., and Woodward, J. *Experiment in Industrial Democracy.* London: Faber and Faber, 1968.

Flanders, A. *Collective Bargaining: Prescription for Change.* London: Faber and Faber, 1967.

_____. *The Fawley Productivity Agreements.* London: Faber and Faber, 1967.

Franz, V.R.W., Holloway, R.G., and Lonergan, W.G. *The Organizational Survey Feedback Principle as a Technique for Encouraging Workers' Involvement in Organization Improvement.* Geneva: International Institute for Labour Studies, 1970.

Furstenburg, G., "Workers' Participation in Management in the Federal Republic of Germany," *International Institute for Labour Studies Bulletin.* Vol. 6, (1969), pp. 94-148.

Garson, G. David, "Some Recent Developments in Workers' Participation in Europe," presented at the National Conference on Workers' Self-Management, Cambridge, Mass., January 12-13, 1974.

Garnett, J. *Democracy in Industry*. London: The Industrial Society, 1976.

_____. *Practical Policies for Participation*. London: The Industrial Society, 1974.

Guest, D., and Fatchett, D. *Worker Participation: Individual Control and Performance*. London: Institute of Personnel Management, 1974.

Harrison, R. *Workers' Participation in Western Europe, 1976*. London: Institute of Personnel Management, 1976.

Hebden, J., and Shaw, G. *Pathways to Participation*. London: Associated Business Programmes Ltd., 1977.

Hunnius, G. *Industrial Democracy and Canadian Labour*. London: Black Rose Books, 1970.

_____. *Participatory Democracy for Canada*. London: Black Rose Books, 1971.

Industrial Labour Organization. *Multinationals in Western Europe: The Industrial Relations Experience*. Geneva: International Labour Office, 1976.

_____. *Participation of Workers in Decisions Within Undertakings*. Labour-Management Series, No. 33, Geneva: International Labour Office, 1970.

_____. *Workers Participation in Decisions Within Undertakings*. Labour-Management Series, No. 48, Geneva: International Labour Office, 1974.

_____. *Report on the International Seminar on Workers' Participation in Decisions Within Undertakings*. Geneva: International Labour Office, 1970.

Jacques, E. *The Changing Culture of a Factory*. London: Tavistock, 1951.

Jenkins, D. *Job Power, Blue and White Collar Democracy*. Garden City, New York: Doubleday Books, 1973.

Kendrick, J.W. *Understanding Productivity*. Baltimore: The Johns Hopkins University Press, 1977.

Likert, R. *The Human Organization*. New York: McGraw-Hill, 1967.

Lloyd, G., and Cannell. *Workers' Participation in Decisions Within Undertakings in the United Kingdom*. Geneva: International Labour Office, 1974.

Macbeath, I. *Power Sharing in Industry*. London: Gower Press, 1975.

_____. *The European Approach to Worker-Management Relations*. British-North American Committee, 1973.

McCarthy, W.E.S., and Ellis, N.D. *Management by Agreement: An Alternative to the Industrial Relations Act*. London: Hutchinson, 1973.

McGregor, D. *The Human Side of Enterprise*. New York: McGraw-Hill, 1960.

Malles, P. *Trends in Industrial Relations Systems in Continental Europe*. Study No. 7, Task Force on Labour Relations, Ottawa: Queen's Printer, 1970.

Maslow, A.H. *Motivation and Personality*. New York: Harper and Row, 1954.

National Center for Productivity and Quality of Working Life. *Recent Initiatives in Labor-Management Cooperation*. Washington, D.C.: U.S. Government Printing Office, 1976.

Newton, K. *The Theory and Practice of Industrial Democracy: A Canadian Perspective*. Discussion Paper No. 94, Ottawa: Economic Council of Canada, August, 1977.

Paul, W.S., and Robertson, K.B. *Job Enrichment and Employee Motivation*. London: Gower Press, 1971.

Poole, M. *Workers' Participation in Industry*. London: Routledge and Kegan Paul, 1971.

Pritchard, B.L.(ed.). *Industrial Democracy in Australia*. CCH Australia Ltd., 1976.

Radice, G., ed. *Working Power*. Fabian Tract 431, London: The Fabian Society, 1974.

Roach, John M. *Worker Participation: New Voices in Management*. New York: The Conference Board, 1973.

Roberts, B.C. *Industrial Democracy - The Challenge to Management*. Institute of Personnel Management National Conference, October, 1976.

Roberts, Ernie. *Workers' Control*. London: Allen and Unwin, 1973.

Ross, Arthur M., "Prosperity and Labor Relations in Europe: the Case of Western Germany," *Quarterly Journal of Economics*, Vol. 76, No. 3, August 1962.

Secretariat, Commission of the European Communities, "Proposed Statute for the European Community," Supplement to the *Bulletin of the European Communities (1970)*. No. 8, pp. 87-122.

Sanderson, G., ed. *A New Role For Labour: Industrial Democracy Today*. Toronto: McGraw-Hill Ryerson, 1979.

Shutt, H., ed. *Worker Participation in West Germany, Sweden, Yugoslavia and the United Kingdom*. London: The Economist Intelligence Unit, 1975.

Sturmthal, A., "Bullock and the Aftermath," *Industrial Relations*. Laval University, Vol. 32, No., 3, 1977, p. 299.

_____, "Workers' Participation in Management: A Review of United States Experience," *International Institute for Labor Studies Bulletin*, Geneva, June 1969, 6, pp. 149-186.

_____. *Workers' Councils*. Cambridge, Mass.: Harvard University Press, 1964.

Tabb, J.Y., and Goldfarb, A. *Workers' Participation in Management: Expectations and Experience*. Elmsford, N.Y.: Pergamon, 1970.

Thomason, G.F., "Workers' Participation in Private Enterprise Organizations," in Balfour, C., *Participation in Industry*, London: Croom Helm, 1973.

Tilden, W.A., "Germany", in *Worker Participation: The European Experience*, Coventry: Coventry and District Engineering Employers' Association, 1974.

Vaneck, J., ed. *Self-Management: Economic Liberation of Man*. Harmondsworth, Middx.: Penguin Books Ltd., 1975.

Walker, K.F. *Workers' Participation in Management: An International Perspective*. Geneva: International Institute for Labour Studies, 1972.

Wall, T.D., and Lischeron, J.A. *Worker Participation: A Critique of the Literature and Some Fresh Evidence*. London: McGraw Hill, 1977.

Webb, G.H. *Participation - Myth or Reality*. Geneva: International Labour Office, 1974.

Wellens, J. *Worker Participation: A Practical Policy*. Guilsborough: Wellens Publishing, 1975.

Wertheim, Edward G., "The Impact of European Worker Participation Schemes on Managerial Decision Making," *Proceedings of the Northeast Aids Meeting*. April, 1975.

_____, "Worker Participation and Industrial Relations," *Industrial Relations*. Laval University, Vol. 31, No. 1, 1976, p.98.

U.K. Government Publications:

Report of the Committee of Inquiry on Industrial Democracy, Cmnd., 6706, H.M.S.O., London, January, 1977. (Bullock Report).

N.A.B. Wilson, "On the Quality of Working LIfe," D.E. Manpower, Paper No. 7, H.M.S.O., 1973.

Industrial Democracy, Cmnd. 7231, H.M.S.O., London, 1978.

Commission on Industrial Relations. *Worker Particiipation and Collective Bargaining in Europe*. H.M.S.O., London, 1974.

Trade Union and Political Publications.
Labour Party. *Industrial Democracy*. Working Party Report, 1967.
Liberal Party. *Opportunity Knocks*. New Direction No. 4, Plan for
    Partnership.
Industrial Democracy. Interim Report by the T.U.C. General Council,
    1975.
Industrial Democracy. T.U.C., July 1974.
Report of a Working Group of the Labour Party Industrial Policy
    Sub-Committee. *The Community and the Company: Reform of
    Company Law*. London, The Labour Party, 1974.

O.E.C.D. Publications:
Work in a Changing Industrial Society. Paris: OECD, 1974.
Prospects for Labour Management Co-Operation in the Enterprise.
    Paris: OECD, 1975.
Workers' Participation. Paris: OECD, 1975.
Changes in Labour-Management Relations in the Enterprise. Paris:
    OECD, 1975, by N.F. Dufty.
Participation and Manpower Policy. Paris: OECD, 1969, by
    F.J. Stendenbach.
"The Emerging Attitudes and Motivations of Workers: Report of a
    Management Experts' Meeting," Paris, May 24-26, 1971, Paris,
    OECD, 1972.

Articles of Special Interest to Canadian Readers:
The Labour Gazette. Labour Canada, Ottawa.
Albeda, W., "Confidentiality and Conflict of Loyalty," Aug. 76,
    p. 44.
Anton, F.R., "Worker Directors and Company Law," Nov. 77,
    p. 495.
Bandeen, R.A., "Workers on the Board - It's Only a Matter of Time,"
    Oct. 76, p. 531.
Banks, J., "The Worker Director and Role Conflict," Nov. 77,
    p. 501.
Bannon, A., "The Co-determination Question in Canada - Some
    Feedback," Dec. 76, p. 661.
Blanpain, R., "Worker Participation - A Varied Concept," Sept. 76,
    p. 470.
Brown, J., "Occupational Health and Safety: The Importance of
    Worker Participation," April 78, p. 123.
Clarke, J., "The Social and Historical Roles of Co-determination in
    West Germany," Aug. 76, p. 432.

Connaghan, C., "Co-determination - a Partial Answer to Good Labour Relations," Aug. 76, p. 405.

Cunningham, C., "The Adversary System is Here to Stay," Oct. 76, p. 542.

Davies, R.J., "Industrial Democracy in Europe and Its Relevance for Canada: A Critical Review," April 78, p. 133.

_____, "The Role and Relevance of Theory in Industrial Relations," Oct. 77, p. 436.

Donahue, T.R., "Current Trends in U.S. Industrial Relations - Why U.S. Unions Reject Co-determination," Sept. 76, p. 473.

Dufour, G., "Canada Cannot Import German-style Co-determination," January, 1977, p. 9.

Elling, K.A., "Co-determination by Decree is not a Panacea," Oct. 76. p. 533.

Finn, E., "In Praise of Participation," Jan. 77, p.5.

Furstenberg, F., "Workers' Participation - The European Experience," Aug. 76, p. 424.

Hammarstrom, O., "Negotiation for Co-determination - the Swedish Model," Oct. 76. p. 535.

_____, "On Participation in Sweden," Reprint from *Sweden Now,* Oct. 1976, p. 538.

_____, "Employees on the Board: the Views of Two Swedish Businessmen," Reprint from *Sweden Now,* Oct. 76, p. 541.

Malles, P., "Co-determination in Canada: What Forms Should It Take?" Aug. 76, P. 415.

Pascal, J., "Mitbestimmung - Kanada? or Would West German 'Co-determination' Work Here?" Aug. 76. p. 408.

Rumball, D., "Worker Participation in Canada?" Aug. 76, p. 429.

Vennat, P., "Worker Participation - Some Views From Quebec," Oct. 76, p. 450.

Vollmer, R.J., "Industrial Democracy West German Style," Aug. 76, p. 421.

Wilson, H.B., Levine, G., Rowley, R.K., and Hunnius, G., "Prospects for Industrial Democracy in Canada: Four Views," Aug. 76, p. 436.

Alexander, K.O., "On Work and Authority: Issues in Job Enlargement, Job Enrichment, Worker Participation, and Shared Authority," *American Journal of Economics and Sociology,* Vol. 34, No. 1, January 1975, pp. 42-54.

Anglo-German Foundation. *The Approach to Industrial Change in Britain and Germany.* London, 1979.

Arndt, Sorge, "The Evolution of Industrial Democracy in the Countries of the European Community," *British Journal of Industrial Relations,* Vol. XIV, No. 3, November 1976.

Greenberg, Edward S., "The Consequences of Worker Participation: A Clarification of the Theoretical Literature," *Social Science Quarterly,* Vol. 56, No. 52, September 1975, pp. 190-209.

Kwoka, J.E. Jr., "The Organization of Work: A Conceptual Framework," *Social Science Quarterly,* Vol. 57, No. 3, 1976, pp. 632-643.

Preston, L.E., and Post, J.E., "The Third Managerial Revolution," *Academy of Management Journal,* Vol. 17, No. 3, Sept. 1974, pp. 476-486.

Rumball, D., "Should Workers Help Run Your company?" *The Financial Post Management,* April 10, 1976.

"The Workers at the Boardroom Door," *The Economist,* Sept. 4, 1976.

"Workers on the Board", *The Economist,* March 24, 1973.

Walker, K.F., "Workers Participation in Management. Concepts and Reality," in Barratt, B., Rhodes, E., and Beishon, J., (eds.), *Industrial Relations,* London: Collier-MacMillan, 1975.

Weinberg, E., "Labor-Management Cooperation: A Report on Recent Initiatives *Monthly Labor Review,* Washington, D.C.: U.S. Dept. of Labor, April 1976.

White, T.H., "Worker Attitudes about Industrial Democracy," *The Canadian Personnel and Industrial Relations Journal,* Sept. 72, pp. 39-42.